YOUR

FASHION

~~DREAM~~

PLAN

Turn your career dream into reality.
An empowering actionable plan to break
into the fashion industry.

GIADA GRAZIANO

GO Publishing

Published by GO Publishing of Glam Observer S.r.l.
Illustrations and Cover Design by Giada Graziano
Editor Jennifer Duardo

ISBN ebook 9788894562828
ISBN Hardcover 9788894562842
ISBN Paperback 9788894562804

FIRST EDITION
ENGLISH EDITION

www.glamobserver.com

For all the fashion enthusiasts who wake up everyday saying:
"My dream is to work in fashion."

Don't let it be just a dream. You can make it come true.

Become the fashion designer, editor, buyer, merchandiser, stylist, publicist, art director... that you are meant to be.

You already have what it takes.

To Ivan and my family for the support
over the years.

To all of you who have been part of the
Glam Observer world even once in these six years.

A special thank you to all my students and
members.

CONTENTS

Introduction

I don't remember exactly when I realized I wanted to work in fashion. It would probably seem more interesting and cliché if I told you that I had been dreaming of working in fashion since the age of six when I was playing with my mom's clothes or while reading *Vogue* in middle school; I liked clothes but I don't remember ever saying "I want to work in fashion" in those early years. I was fourteen when the cult movie *The Devil Wears Prada* was released, and as for most fashion lovers, it has also become one of my favorite movies. I bought the book and I also devoured *Confessions of a Shopaholic* released a couple of years later, as well as other movies and books with references to the world of fashion. If I think back to how I loved those films and watched them until I knew the scenes by heart, I could say today that surely something was sparked in those years. However, I remember very well that when I had to choose what to study at university, I wanted to work in beauty and create makeup and skincare products. Besides fashion, I had a great passion for beauty, one of the main reasons being that my acne had made me obsessed with finding the perfect products to remove it and cover it with makeup. It was also the time of the first beauty tutorials on YouTube, especially in America, and I was fascinated. I'd gotten pretty good at doing my own makeup as well as my friends', and became an expert in skincare and what products to use, just by following the advice of YouTube girls. But this could be a topic for another book, we're not here to talk about makeup but rather a career in fashion!

So, I had to decide which degree program to enroll in. Out of indecision, I did something that, without knowing it, is one of the most useful strategies that I still share among all of the different career advice I give to those who want to work in fashion. I sent an email to Chanel, Dior, L'Oréal, Sephora, and other beauty companies and labs asking which degree they would consider when hiring someone to work in their companies. I went to their websites, found their email addresses and emailed them. I didn't think they would ever answer me, but I had nothing to lose. After a couple of weeks, Dior and Chanel got back to me saying who they typically hired to work in their cosmetic laboratories. A response from these big companies! I was amazed and excited.

In contacting those companies I didn't know that I was doing something very useful for my career: putting myself out there and asking for what I wanted. I was taking action. I was going out of my comfort zone.

When I think about that episode today, I still smile and congratulate my younger self for having sent those emails without anyone guiding me.

As a fashion career expert and coach today, there is not one day that I don't share this advice with someone: send that email to get want you want, don't wait for a job to get posted, put yourself out there.

Although I don't remember the exact moment when I first realized my desire to get into the fashion industry, I remember the enthusiasm of wanting to be part of it, which was getting stronger. I don't remember *when* I decided to work in fashion but *how much* I wanted to do it once I did it. I dreamed about working in a beautiful fashion office every time I [re]watched *The Devil Wears Prada* and being fascinated by the beauty of clothes when watching fashion shows (even before Instagram let anyone be part of the front row).

If you have this book in your hands it's probably because you have these same feelings, and likely that your dream is to obtain a job in fashion.

But when it came time to get serious and think about my

career, along with the excitement, I also remember the feelings of discouragement, of being confused, of struggling about what steps to take to get a job into the fashion industry and how it seemed hard and sometimes impossible to be part of it, especially if you a) didn't have the opportunity to attend a fashion school, b) don't have experience in the industry, c) don't live in a fashion capital, or d) don't have any connections in the industry.

Sound familiar?

I experienced all the good and bad feelings that come with wanting to enter the industry; the excitement but also the discouragement.

I remember those days when I went on the internet to find out more about getting a job in fashion and I couldn't find any valuable information on how to enter the fashion industry or what the different career options were.
I had zero work experience, zero connections, zero education in fashion. I felt lost and I didn't have any idea about what to do to get a job at a fashion company.

I was surprised that Google couldn't give me an answer as I usually rely on it for basically everything. I felt lost but I didn't give up, I still couldn't see myself working in any other industry but fashion. At that time in 2015, the year I graduated (by the way, in the end, I didn't choose to study chemistry as the beauty companies suggested, because I changed my mind about working in beauty /makeup and I chose management engineering instead for reasons I can't remember!) when I was doing my research, all of the links that mentioned careers in fashion were just promoting a fashion school or course.

First takeaway:

Even if you are undecided on what degree to go with, which by the way is totally normal that at eighteen you can't decide what you want to do for the rest of your life, you can still change your mind again after you graduate and enter the industry that you love, as I did! Not all people who want to work in fashion know it from the beginning and then decide to attend a fashion school. Many people get a more "traditional degree" such as communication, journalism, marketing, management, or business and then decide to get into this industry later after they graduate. Even those who dream about working in fashion since they started walking, not all of them can afford a fashion school or necessarily want to attend one and prefer to obtain a traditional degree.

The good news is that whether or not you attend a fashion school, you can be part of the fashion industry! But more on this later in the book.

Today I'm grateful for that struggle. Because if I didn't feel the sadness, the discouragement, or the confusion about what steps to take to get a job in fashion, I would probably not be here writing this book to help you and would not have had the idea of founding the first fashion career advice destination that is Glam Observer.

At that moment, when fashion blogs were quite popular and anyone was starting one just by posting photos of outfits, I decided to start the first one focused on breaking down industry secrets, beginning my mission of making the fashion industry accessible to anyone who wanted to enter it.

What a fun fact that some years ago I was on the other side while today it's my job and business to help all of you who want to enter the fashion industry.

But it's probably the fact that I experienced for myself
- the struggle
- the excitement
- the job search
- the reality of working in fashion (before working on Glam Observer full-time I had a job in fashion e-commerce at YOOX, Net-a-Porter, and Alexander McQueen, that I quit to help you all get a job in fashion!)
- and the knowledge (after graduation I took online courses at FIT and Parsons and moved to Milan for a Master's in Luxury and Fashion Management);
that today I'm able to help so many people from all over the world to break into the fashion industry.

I remember how happy and excited I was on the first day of my first fashion internship. I remember that I was happy because, after all the struggle, I had finally made it.

I want you to feel that same excitement of your first day in a fashion office (without the struggle) and that's why I'm writing this book with the aim of helping you turn your dream into reality, but hopefully saving you some time and a good dose of stress.

Having mentored thousands of fashion industry enthusiasts from around the world over the past five years, I've heard many misconceptions about getting a job in fashion that can be summarized into these:

It's necessary to study fashion
If you don't have the experience you can't get a job
You can't intern if you are not a fashion student
If you don't know anyone in fashion you won't make it
If you've tried to get a job in fashion for a few months with no results, fashion must not be meant for you
I'm not good enough, there are so many people better than me…

THESE STATEMENTS ARE ALL FALSE.

Repeat with me
THESE ARE FALSE

Whoever has been spreading this false information has been doing an effective job, as 98% of the people who want to start a career in fashion (myself included years ago) believe in at least one of these misconceptions.

So, let's make it clear:
It's FALSE that you can't get a job in fashion if you didn't study fashion
It's FALSE that you can't get a job in fashion if you don't have experience yet
It's FALSE that you can't get a job in fashion if you don't know anyone
It's FALSE that the fashion industry is not made for you or that you are not enough for it

These misconceptions are devastating to many people and are also the reason why I do what I do. That's why I've been running a website for five years now, inspiring, motivating, and breaking down the barriers of this industry, revealing its secrets and the truth of what it really takes to enter it.
That's also the reason why I organize fashion panels where I invite fashion industry professionals to tell the true stories about how they got started, and why I created the first and only course (Break into the Fashion Industry) that teaches you

unconventional strategies to make it in this industry.

I'm writing this book to be a wake-up call, a big shoulder-shaking for all of you, to give you a practical plan to break into the fashion industry and turn your fashion dream into reality.

How many times have you crushed or given up a dream because you believed that you couldn't make it? Including that of working in fashion?

Maybe it's because you didn't attend a fashion school, because you don't live in a fashion capital, or because you don't have any experience in this field...

I know these things resonate with many of you. And that's why I'm sitting here now writing this book, to drive and push you, take away the limitations, false beliefs, and misconceptions that are preventing you from getting your dream job in fashion.

It doesn't matter what skills you lack, the connections or experience you don't have or if you attended or didn't attend a fashion course, YOU have the power to work on ALL of these things, you have the power to change and get whatever you want, to acquire the skills you lack, to become the most recognized stylist, publicist, editor, photographer, buyer, journalist, merchandiser, brand manager... to get that dream job at the top company, that promotion, or your first internship even if you start from scratch.

You have the power to completely turn around your life and career.

If you don't believe that inside YOU there is the power to get what you want or are wondering how you can become more confident and take the steps that you need, just stay with me till the end of this book and you'll figure it out.

There are endless books out there for entrepreneurs that teach how to build a million-dollar business. Most of them will tell you that if you want to become a successful entrepreneur, you have to start acting like one and add some specific practices and habits into your daily routines. These authors have spent their lives studying the most successful entrepreneurs and analyzing what they have in common, to build a system that you can replicate if you want to run the next million-dollar business.

What if I tell you that there are some practical things and actions that you can incorporate into your routines, strategies that can help you become the successful fashion industry professional you're meant to be?

I've spent the last six years studying the industry, analyzing the success of the most established industry professionals, interviewing and talking to thousands of people who work in fashion, so I know what you need to start doing to reach that same level of success on your own terms.

I'm a pragmatic person, I do have a rational approach to everything, and I like practical, actionable things. When learning how to do something I like to find that in order to get there I need to follow step 1, step 2 and step 3. I like to take action and to observe the consequences and the results.

That is how I have developed the content of Glam Observer. If you've read a GO article, attended an event, listened to a podcast episode, or if you are a student of one of my online courses, you know that I get straight to the point and suggest the actions to take if you want to network, if you want to succeed at your job interview, if you want to write an exceptional cover letter, or if you want to pitch fashion editors to get your work published.

This book is no different and is as practical and direct as all of the other content I've put out there.

It took me a while to come up with the title of the book, it was clear from the beginning, but I just couldn't see it.

I've chosen *Your Fashion Dream* and I also added the word *Plan* because this is what we are going to do.

There are so many people who wake up everyday saying:

"My dream is to get a job in fashion."

This book is about turning your dream into reality and in order to do so, we won't talk anymore about your dream of getting a job in fashion, but we are going to use the word GOAL, because the latter is what makes the difference between turning it into a reality or not.

A goal, in fact, is a dream but actionable and, taking action together with the right mindset, are the most powerful tools you have to make it happen.

We all have ideas and dreams, but what makes the difference between those who are successful and those who live day by day hoping that something will magically happen, is that the first ones take action.

I hope with this book you'll become one of those who take action to get what you want.

My dream is to get a job in fashion

becomes

My goal is to get a job in fashion

This book is your plan of actions to get where you want to go.

Notice the difference and how it sounds more practical and less an image that just exists in your mind?
If you leave it as just a dream, then it will probably stay there forever, but if you treat it like a goal, your mind and subconscious will start acting *with* you to make it happen.
 You cannot just apply online for a job and hope to get a call back from the company. Hope is not a strategy.
Hope is not what we are going to talk about in this book. Assuming the universe is on your side and that sooner or later you'll get something is pointless. In this book we are going to talk about how you can start taking action, what actions to take,

and the habits to embrace to achieve your fashion dream.

I'm writing this book to unlock your inner potential, give you the strategies, and build your confidence. I believe in you. You have your own skill sets, you are special but maybe you still don't know it, or are not convinced yet.

You will be the next successful editor, buyer, designer, stylist, publicist, merchandiser, publicist… and I'm happy to be a small part of your journey.

You are capable of more than you know.

Ready? Let's get started.

PART I

Misconceptions, lies and myths of the fashion industry to let go of

The things we decide to believe in condition us, even if we don't realize it. We think we are acting to achieve what we want to achieve, but our mind is working unconsciously at the same time, and if we do not let go of some conditions and still believe in what is not true, it is easy for our mind to convince us to act in ways that are the opposite of what we would like to achieve.

What I'm trying to tell you is that <u>if your mind believes you can't do it, then you almost certainly won't.</u>

That's why I decided to start this book by discussing all the misconceptions, myths, and lies related to the fashion industry. Otherwise all of the tips and strategies proposed in this book will almost certainly not work if you continue to believe these things that are an obstacle to you.

Considering these false myths, misconceptions and lie to be true, that they represent reality, is the main obstacle for those who dream of working in fashion, who then give up before even starting. And even for those who don't give up from the beginning, they might not be confident enough and so they will try, closing their eyes with fingers crossed, hoping it will end well. They lack the determination they need to succeed.

I get dozens of emails and messages every day with at least one of these excuses, so let's debunk them once and for all. As I mentioned in the introduction, everything you need to work in fashion is inside you and it all depends on your mindset and what you believe in. If you have a negative mindset and are blocked by false beliefs it will be difficult for you to get what you want. I hope that once you dispel these myths, you will feel more confident and act with a plan and the determination and motivation you need to achieve what you deserve.

1

MISCONCEPTION #*1*
It's necessary to study fashion to work in

I have interviewed many fashion industry professionals over the past few years for Glam Observer. Whether it's a written interview, podcast, or live event, I always ask this question:

"Do you think it is necessary to study fashion to work in this industry?"

The answer from everyone is always "NO". I would like to emphasize that this includes those who work in fashion today and have attended a fashion school as well as those who have a traditional degree.
I want to write it big enough so that you can print it in your head:

IT IS <u>NOT</u> NECESSARY TO STUDY FASHION TO WORK IN THIS INDUSTRY.

Although I am aware of this truth, I still ask this question to every person I interview in order to gather as many opinions as possible. Once I graduated, I was determinate to enter the fashion industry. At that time, I thought that being a girl from southern Italy, where there are no fashion schools and there are no fashion companies, and with my degree in Management Engineering completely unrelated to the industry, my only chance to enter the fashion industry and be considered by companies was to study something related to fashion.

As soon as I dipped my feet into this world with my first internship, I found myself in an office with many people who had a traditional degree and only a few who studied fashion. Definitely not what I expected. I quickly realized that it was not just a coincidence in my office, but in general all fashion companies hire equally, if not more, those with a traditional degree vs. those who studied fashion.

I didn't want to pursue a creative career like the role of designer, but preferred a more analytical role working in e-commerce, management, or merchandising, so my degree in management engineering would have been enough to land my first internship and start a career in fashion. But at that time, a few years ago, I didn't know this. So I decided to enroll in a master's program as if it were a secure ticket to the fashion industry.

Getting a fashion degree is of course useful, but going to fashion school as if it guarantees a job is not the right reason to attend, because in the end, no matter which prestigious university you are attending, it is always YOU who are responsible for what you get.

Although I was studying toward a master's degree, I worked hard to enter the fashion industry, perfecting my resume and my applications. I wasn't waiting for a job opportunity to come to me or for the school to help me get a job. If you don't know yet, most fashion schools are connected with certain fashion companies. Most schools have priority access to job offers which means that oftentimes companies ask the school if they have someone suitable for a job and the school might recommend some students for a job interview. However, this does not mean that you are guaranteed a job. Companies have vacancies available when they need to fill a position, which is not necessarily when students graduate. Furthermore, they will always hire the best candidate based on their needs, so if they feel that the school's recommendation is not the right one, they will choose someone else.

That's why even those who study fashion must put in a lot of their own effort to enter this industry and learn the correct way to apply for a job in fashion.

So to return to the main topic, I think education is the best investment you can make for yourself. Even today I continue to attend online courses, read books, and get informed every day (I think self-education can be even more profitable). So I'm not here to advise against taking fashion courses. If you are attending a fashion school, that's great! I just hope you are doing it for the right reasons: to learn about fashion and to get in touch with industry professionals, and not the wrong one: believing it is your only chance to find a job in fashion.

My message here is that even if you have studied something else, if you do not want to or cannot attend a fashion course, you can still work in this industry.

Not everyone can afford a fashion school and this doesn't have to be a discriminating factor that prevents people from pursuing their dream of working in fashion. Many others realize they want to enter the industry when they have already chosen a different degree. What about them? Should one give up just because at age eighteen and pressured with choosing a university they didn't have a clear idea of what they wanted to do for the rest of their life? Obviously not.

I admire people who have clear ideas from the beginning, but in most cases, one is too young and inexperienced to understand what career path will bring the most satisfaction. I went from wanting to graduate in chemistry and produce beauty products, to a degree in management engineering, then working in fashion, and finally quitting everything to start my own business! Changing ideas is absolutely normal and I think it is necessary to say that *you can move from one dream to another.*

So, let's break down this first barrier: if you didn't go and you don't have plans to attend a fashion school, you can still be part of this industry.

You can become a stylist, buyer, work in PR or marketing, or work at a fashion magazine without having studied fashion. You've learned Excel and the 7Ps of marketing with your economics degree, you acquired writing skills in your literature courses, and, on graduation day, even if you have no fashion experience, you can still work in the industry! We all had to learn what it takes with practice. So who says that a degree in economics, communication, or literature is not enough to work in fashion?

There is only one career that could be an exception to all the others in fashion: the fashion designer.

The technical skills of drawing, pattern making, and transforming a dress from a model paper into a prototype, are taught only in a fashion school. And it's also the career in which a fashion degree is usually required in the job listing.

Even so, if you want to become a designer but can't attend fashion school, don't underestimate the power of self-education through Google, books, online courses, and YouTube videos. In the end, fashion companies look at the portfolio and work when hiring a designer; if you can build a strong portfolio because you have learned how to sketch and design beautiful clothes by watching YouTube videos and you have extraordinary talent, then you win!

Remember that an unconventional and creative application can overcome the lack of skills and experience required for a job in any career, including that of the designer.

.

When companies require a fashion-related degree as a main

requirement, you have two options:

1. Apply anyway by presenting a great portfolio that demonstrates that you have the skills despite not having studied fashion, together with a convincing cover letter and an unconventional application (more about these in the next chapters).

2. Move on to the next job offer. Just because a few jobs you found required a degree in fashion, it doesn't mean it's the rule and that all companies require one. There are many prestigious brands that do not consider a degree in fashion to be mandatory. Start with these and once you have the necessary experience, you can move to other companies if that's what you want. In fashion, experience matters more than what you studied, so gain experience in companies where they don't require a degree in fashion and then you can move to another company.

Attending a fashion school has many advantages, but luckily there are many things you can do yourself to fill the gaps of not having attended one.

1. One of the greatest advantages of attending a fashion school is meeting people who work in fashion during your classes: editors, stylists, managers ... But today, thanks to the internet and social media, we ALL have access to everyone. It has never been easier to connect with anyone from anywhere in the world. So even if you don't connect with these fashion professionals through your school, you can do the work yourself and connect with these people via Instagram or LinkedIn. We will see later in another chapter how you can network with fashion industry professionals such as buyers, editors, designers ... and contact them even only to ask questions about their careers.

2. When you attend a fashion school, all of your classmates have a passion and interest for this sector and therefore you have a group of people you can talk to and exchange daily opinions on the fashion industry. When I decided I wanted to work in fashion, I was studying management engineering and none of my classmates were interested in working in fashion. So I missed someone to talk about fashion with and share the job search process. With no connections I felt even more left out of this industry than I already was.

That's why, when I decided to launch Glam Observer and support all those who want to work in fashion, one of the first things I thought about was creating an international online community where people could exchange opinions, feel like they are already part of fashion even without having a job in it, congratulate each other on successes, and also support each other in difficult times.

I'm happy that today people who have studied fashion and those who don't are part of the GO community, so it's super interesting to have this mix and get to hear different opinions. Being a global community, many Glam Observer members bond and meet in person in various cities to go to fashion exhibitions together, photograph a project for their portfolio, exchange job opportunities, and more. So even if you didn't go to fashion school, you can join a community and find other fashion enthusiasts like yourself who speak the same fashion language, receive updates about job offers, get ideas on careers that you didn't consider... basically these are the fashion classmates that you never had.

3. An obvious aspect of those attending a fashion school is that all classes and projects are fashion-focused: writing for the school's fashion magazine, organizing a photo shoot, the final show to showcase your collection ... but you can have all of these experiences even if you are not taking fashion classes or if your fashion school does not offer programs like these (not all the fashion schools have practical activities like these, so if you are considering a fashion school check out reviews but also the workshops and other activities offered outside the classroom). You can always have a similar experience yourself by starting your own online or print fashion magazine or starting your own blog. You can find other fashion enthusiasts on Instagram or in a fashion community and work together on a photo shoot or you can even organize your own fashion show! Find other young models and student stylists who want to build their own portfolio and create something together. Thanks to the internet, anyone can create their own experience. Everything you need is just a click away.

In fashion it seems that people are more competitive with each other than in any other industry, but there is nothing better than putting multiple heads together to create something extraordinary. Collaboration over competition is key. You will benefit a lot from working with other colleagues.

11

Learning about the industry is very important. Even if you didn't go to fashion school, you can learn a lot by reading books, listening to podcasts, watching videos on YouTube, and attending online courses (definitely cheaper and no less interesting).

It's important to keep up-to-date with what's happening in the industry by reading the daily news from sites like Business of Fashion, WWD, Fashionista.com, Vogue, Glam Observer ;)

At this point I hope I have convinced you that you can work in fashion, even if you have not studied fashion, and I imagine you are wondering how.

The answer is actually very simple. There is one thing that everyone who wants to work in fashion, regardless of the department they want to enter (pr, design, purchasing, merchandising, etc) and what they have studied (fashion or not), must start: fashion internships.

In the six years that I have interviewed and spoken with buyers, editors, designers, CEOs, and stylists, I have learned that they all started their careers in fashion through internships.

Think of any name in the industry you admire, any designer or editor, and if you ask or do some research, you'll find they started with an internship.

We will discuss in the next chapters everything about fashion internships and how to get one. The goal of this chapter was to debunk the myth and convince you that you can get an internship and work in fashion even without a fashion degree.

2

MISCONCEPTION #2
I Have No Fashion Experience; I'll Never Find Work In This Industry

Wondering if it's necessary to study fashion to work in this industry and being convinced that it is true, is something that I can understand. And not only because it was a conviction that I also had, but because this is what society tells us. They say that you have to study engineering to become an engineer, medicine to become a doctor, and law to become a lawyer. So logically it is easy to assume that the same applies to fashion since there are specialized courses and schools. We have just seen in the previous chapter how this logic does not apply to fashion.

But when I hear or read: "I can't find a job in fashion" or "I can't work in fashion, because I don't have experience in the industry," this doesn't sound like an assumption based on logic, right?

Have you ever stopped to wonder how the best designers, stylists, and editors got started? They were not born with experience already on their CV. They all started from scratch, with a resume that consisted only of a degree, and for some, not even that.

It goes without saying that not everyone will get a full-time job in fashion as soon as you decide that you want one. Because before getting a job there is one step you need to take that will get you the experience you need.

So, Giada, what's the point here?

Someone says: "That job as a Buyer / PR / Stylist… required 1-2 years of experience and I worked in a store while I was studying so
I applied, but they didn't hire me."
Well, working in a store isn't quite the same thing. When they are looking for a person with 1-2 years of experience, they mean they are looking for someone who has experience in a similar role.

You'd be surprised to know how many people can't find a job just because they're applying for the wrong one. They don't read the job description carefully.

It's easy to be fooled by the word "junior" or "assistant," but if you pay attention and read who the company is looking for, you can see that most of these "entry-level" jobs actually require a minimum experience of 1-2 years.

There is an interesting Harvard Business Review article that analyzes a report released by HP in which it was found that women do not apply for a job if they are not 100% qualified. Men apply when they have 60% of the requirements.

What is interesting to know is that Tara Sophia Mohr, author of that article, did a survey and found that in reality, both women and men do not apply for a job not because they lack self-confidence. In fact, 41% of women and 46% of men said that the main reason for not applying is: "I didn't think they would hire me because I didn't have the qualifications and I didn't want to waste time and energy."

Big mistake.

First of all, because you never know what a company might think about you. They might give more weight to a requirement that you have than to the one that you don't have. Why give up before even starting? Each fashion company evaluates candidates in different ways.

Secondly, you should never wait to meet all the requirements to apply for a job or internship.

Do you remember what I told you in the previous chapter?

An unconventional and creative application can overcome the

lack of skills and experience required for a job in any career, including that of the designer.

We will talk about this later in more detail.

If it is true that you do not have to wait until you meet all the requirements to apply, there is one thing that you should pay attention to: the years of experience required.

This does not mean that if you have found a job that you like and it requires three years of experience that you don't have, you need to give up this career option. You just need to find the "level" that suits your experience.

Example:
Let's say you are excited because you have just found an open position as Fashion Designer Assistant that interests you. Don't assume that just because it has the word Assistant it means it is made for you because you have just graduated. Read the years of experience required in the job listing. If the company requires two years of experience in a similar role, rather than applying with a slim chance of getting the role because you lack experience or worse, getting discouraged and giving up, look for an internship (your level) for that same job in Fashion Design, even in the same company,

Considering the years of experience required does not mean

giving up a role when you don't meet them but looking for a similar role at your level.

So even if you have zero previous experience, there is still an option at your level: fashion internships. Fashion internships are essential if you want to enter the fashion industry and have no or little experience, whether you studied fashion or not. Internships are the work experience for students, recent graduates, and those with little work experience.

Nearly everyone who works in fashion started with internships. Think of any name in fashion and they started from an internship. Diane Von Furstenberg? Internship. Anna Wintour? Internship.

I invite you to search for a name on Google, read an interview, or visit their LinkedIn profile to see how they got started and see how very few people didn't start with an internship.

The university you decide to attend is not your ticket to the fashion industry, fashion internships are. No matter what prestigious school you are attending, you will have to go through internships to acquire the necessary experience to get a full-time job.

Therefore, if it is true that people with degrees in economics, literature, finance, fashion, marketing, management, communication and even those who have no degree at all can work in fashion ... there is one thing in common for anyone who wants to work in the sector: starting from one or even more fashion internships.

What if you have no experience in fashion but have it in another industry?

Of course internships are not for everyone. There are those who have no experience in fashion but have it in another sector. There are many people who decide later in life that they want to change sector or both industry and role.

If you fall into one of these two categories it may be difficult to find an internship, however you can still work in fashion. In fact, you can transfer your previous skills and experience to the fashion industry.

For example, if you worked in marketing at a tech company, you can apply for marketing jobs in fashion. If you are a lawyer, you could work in the legal department of a fashion company.

Over the past recent years, it became increasingly common for fashion companies to hire people from other industries and vice versa. Do you remember Angela Ahrendts who went from being the CEO of Burberry to working at Apple in 2014 where she stayed until 2019? Or Ian Rogers who came from Apple Music with no previous fashion experience when he became LVMH's Chief Digital Officer?

When moving from another industry to fashion, you must above all leverage the cover letter (which we will talk about in the following chapters) by explaining what your previous experiences have in common with fashion and why you would be the right person.

When you change industries but keep the same role, the transition is easier.

When you instead want to change both industry and role things might get trickier. For example, a lawyer who wants to become a stylist, or a financial advisor who wants to become a designer. In these cases, even if you have many years of work experience in an industry, you are starting from zero knowledge in your new career of fashion, so it is impossible to maintain the same level of seniority. Thus, if you are at a senior level in finance, you cannot get a senior job as a designer or stylist because you lack the years of experience and skills of this new role. But if you're willing to start over to pursue this new passion, you can definitely do it!

Changing both role and industry is certainly more challenging, but worth it if you've found your passion.

When the company hires a student or someone young, they know that their work experience could be nonexistent or fall short, so they tend to focus on other factors to evaluate a candidate.

On the other hand, when a recruiter is faced with a candidate that has years of experience, they will focus on understanding your experience in your previous role or industry.

If you want to change both role and industry at the same time (or example, you want to go from working in the marketing department of a technology company to becoming a stylist in fashion), you could consider this trick. Rather than considering a change of industry and career at the same time and taking a giant step, you could change the industry first and then the role. So, start by moving from working in marketing for a technology company to working in marketing for a fashion company, in order to make this transition easily. Once you join a fashion company, you are gaining the industry experience you need. Furthermore, as soon as you join a fashion company, you will begin to meet new people, talk to them, and make the role transition come more naturally, in small steps.

At this point, we have learned that internships can be used by practically anyone who wants to enter the fashion industry and has no or little experience yet—even those who studied fashion or those without a degree. We will delve into them throughout the book.

3

THE LIE
I'm Not Good Enough to Get A Job at The Top Fashion Companies

The two misconceptions we just discussed—that you need to study fashion and you need to have fashion-related work experience to get a job—result in a lack of self-confidence. Many are convinced that they are not good enough, that they will never be able to get a job in the company of their dreams, that they have to "settle" because it is so unattainable, because they have not studied fashion, or have no experience.

But even when I've managed to convince you of the fact that you can work in fashion regardless of your career path and what you've studied, there is still something else that blocks you: the belief that you are not enough for this industry and that you'll never get where you want to be.

"I'm not good enough to get a job at Gucci. They will never consider me."

If you ever thought something similar you can be defined as someone with a scarcity mindset, according to the experts, which refers to a belief that there is not enough abundance for everyone to go around. You may believe that there aren't enough jobs, enough opportunities, enough happiness for everyone, or that you can't get or deserve the best there is out there.

You look at those who work in fashion and it seems that everyone knows their stuff: stylists, editors, buyers, successful designers … You admire them thinking that it is impossible for you to reach their level of success.

Now I want you to think about something. How many stylists, buyers, designers, photographers, or fashion houses are there?

Imagine if each of them had stopped and said: "There are already so many stylists who curate the looks of celebrities, so many designers who create beautiful collections, or so many editors who write interesting articles." They wouldn't have founded the brands we love so much today, we wouldn't see fashion photographed by different eyes, and we'd read a single fashion magazine by a few editors. We would not have that variety of talent and creativity that characterizes the fashion industry.

Yes it's true, there are already many people who do the job you would like to do and work in your favorite companies, but none are like you. Why should you deprive companies of your skills, talent, and personality?

Don't tell me you don't have the talent. It does not represent the truth! None of the people in fashion started directly at this level of success. No, not even Anna Wintour. All the iconic fashion brands you know today—Dior, Chanel, Valentino, Gucci—did not start with the success they have today. Overnight success doesn't exist. They became the successful people and brands you know today after years of experience and lessons learned from their failures. You can be one of them. You have everything you need right now to get started.

It's time for you to identify and destroy this huge lie that is stopping you.

As you might recall, I also thought I wasn't enough when I decided I wanted to enter the fashion industry and ended up in a master's program because of this fear. I know what it feels like and what I'm telling you now, I wish I knew a few years ago. Even now as I write this book I think, "Who do you think you are to write this book?"Many times with Glam Observer I thought I was not good enough to keep the business going. But if I had let the fear of not being enough stop me, I wouldn't be receiving emails and messages from girls and boys thanking me because their life has changed, telling me they've gained self-confidence and now work at the companies of their dreams.

This fills my heart.

But then, who defines who is enough and for what?

I am saddened and angry every time I hear people say they are not enough and give up from the beginning and do not apply to jobs or do what it takes to reach a goal (if we were face to face every time I hear things like this I would shake your shoulders very hard!).

Most of these beliefs we create and misconceptions are perpetuated by society and especially the media. We are all exposed to the lives of other people. Whenever we scroll through our Instagram feeds, we tend to compare ourselves to others, create self-pressure and mental misconceptions. And you know we scroll many times every day! Stop doing it. Stop assuming that others are living their best life and you can't. That they are more qualified than you because they work in the best companies or have the best clients. You too can get your dream job. Which, by the way, in the following chapters we will talk about how the dream job is just a myth!

The next time you scroll through your Instagram feed and you see people working at the best companies or stylists working with the most popular celebrities, a journalist writing for the best magazines, instead of comparing yourself to them and think that they are lucky, and that you are not and you can never do the same because you are not enough, go to LinkedIn or Google and study their career path. See where they started and how they got to where they are today.

This exercise will not only help you understand that they too started from scratch like everyone else, but you will understand how they did it, so you have some sort of path to follow.

Did they do two internships and work in the magazine's closet before publishing their first fashion article? Were they fashion assistants for a year before becoming Junior Editors?

See where you are now and what steps you are missing. If you have one internship at your back and expect to become an editor and are discouraged because you can't find a job as an editor, instead of thinking that you are not enough, maybe the problem is just because you are trying to get to a position by skipping other steps? Maybe you miss that year as Fashion Assistant that today's Fashion Editors did before getting to the current role?

This exercise should help you to stop comparing yourself with others and to think that you are not enough and to make you understand how long and what steps it takes to reach a certain role.

Because no one in fashion has gotten to where they are today overnight. It is a process. The editor you see on Instagram and with whom you tend to compare yourself did not arrive where she is today directly as soon as she graduated, but it took years and various steps.

Yes, there are some people who got there because they knew a friend of a friend, or their parents moved mountains for them, but most people started from scratch with no connections and have built their way up to a wonderful career simply because they believed in themselves and worked hard.

Successful people shouldn't push you to compete with them, but motivate and inspire you to become the version of yourself you've always wanted to be. The next time, rather than comparing your career to someone else's, learn from it, use it as a guide to figure out what the next steps are.

In some cases we allow ourselves to be influenced by the opinions of others. It doesn't matter if it was your mother, sister, best friend, school bully, colleague, boss, or a recruiter at a job interview who told you weren't good enough at this or that ... if you let their thoughts affect your life, you will remain in the same situation and you will not be able to get what you really want. Don't let someone else's opinions block you. Don't let your negative opinions and self-doubt do that either.

Having confidence in yourself doesn't mean not being afraid. It means feeling anxiety and being scared, but deciding to do it anyway.

I want to give you another example to prove that you are good enough as you are now.

At the end of the *Break into the Fashion Industry* course, the student has not acquired a new technical skill and has not even gained new work experience. The course teaches application strategies, networking, etc., so it's not like taking a Photoshop course where you learn a new program and acquire a specific skill needed for a job. So how is it that the student couldn't get a job in fashion before the course and they can immediately after? As much as I would like to, I still can't perform magic. It all depends on how you present yourself to companies and other people. At the end of the course the students have the same skills, education, and work experience as before, but what has changed is the way they start applying to jobs and above all, they stopped being afraid of a list of requirements, they stopped believing that they are not enough, and, as a result, everything changes in just one weekend.

If you believe in yourself, others will believe in you too. If you thought you weren't good enough before the course, you shouldn't have been good enough after, yet companies respond to your applications and you'll soon enter the fashion world.

When I was in my masters program and we were towards the end of classes looking for internships, we all had more or less the same level of experience on our CVs: a traditional degree, not related to fashion, and then all the same masters degree. It happened that 3 or 4 of us were candidates for the same position. Although the company had 3-4 CVs with similar experiences in front of them, in the end they only chose one of us. This is to reinforce that the way you prepare your CV, the way in which you apply, and how you present yourself at the interview, makes all the difference. So if you've been applying for jobs and still haven't received a response, the problem may be with your CV, or how you are applying, it's not necessarily that you are not the right person for that job.

You do not have control over what a company thinks of you. But you have control over the way you create your CV, write your emails, and talk to industry professionals.

When you are sure you have created an attractive resume and a winning cover letter, giving up and not applying to a job out of fear is the biggest mistake you can make. Every job you don't apply for is a lost opportunity.

I remember when I did my first fashion panel in London, I was terrified of the language. I am a native Italian speaker, and I was afraid that sooner or later I would have a mental block and not be able to answer any questions in English. I thought I wasn't good enough until the event ended. Organizing an event abroad in London was something I really wanted to do. I did not allow this self-doubt and fear to stop me. I felt the fear, I felt it from when I started organizing it and looking for speakers, until the last person left that evening. I was terrified, but I did it anyway. My English is fluent today but I still make mistakes because it is not my first language. I don't let that stop me from doing what I like. I've always wanted Glam Observer to be an international platform and community, so I knew right away that I had to speak and write in English to reach more people. Every time I record a podcast I think I might get stuck or that I won't know what to say to the interviewee because of the language. But I do it and in the end, even if my English wasn't perfect in one episode or during my speech, who says it's better not doing it at all so I can avoid any mistakes? When people leave our events they are always happy, inspired, and motivated and I will not let a few emails telling me that my English was horrible stop me from organizing events abroad or recording podcasts. I will continue to study, I will continue to improve myself, but I do not want to wait until I am perfect to start.

No one is perfect, the only person you should compare yourself with is the person you were yesterday.

Being enough as you are does not mean having the presumption of thinking "I know it all." Being enough does not mean settling for what you have in that moment if you are aware that something needs improvement.

English has always been a skill I have focused on, not only with Glam Observer.

When I had to apply for jobs in fashion, I knew that English would be essential. To increase the chances of getting a job and also to feel more confident in my applications, I decided to study English on my own. I started reading books, watching videos, and listening to podcasts in English. Over time I became quite fluent.

Many ask me if to work abroad it is necessary to know the language of that country. Well, of course, I don't need to tell you that if they receive your CV and you also know their language, you certainly have a better chance of getting the job. The point is that even if you don't speak a single word of that language today, apply, write in your CV that you are at a basic level but that you are studying it and you will be fluent shortly, and start learning the language.

Being aware of a limitation should not make you hesitant to move forward, but it should motivate you to get what you need to reach the final goal.

When I had to learn how to build the website, launch the podcast, and create the first course, I learned everything online from Google, books, videos, and podcasts. Even when I had to write this book, I did a lot of research. It is absolutely normal not to have all the necessary skills every time, but <u>there is nothing more beautiful than being a proactive person who can recognize what is missing and work hard to understand how to achieve the goal.</u>

Today we are so lucky to have the internet where you can learn anything. So, if you want to work as a buyer and Excel is required, don't give up just because you don't know how to use Excel. Apply and learn it before the interview: read articles, watch tutorials on YouTube, buy a book.

Any limit can be overcome.
Take control of your life. Don't sit idle.

Just because you don't have a job right now, see it as a "not yet."
You don't have a job yet, but you are going to get one.
Think of how impossible it seemed for you to graduate when you were in your first year of college, yet here you are with a degree in hand. Think about when you had to do something that seemed difficult, but in the end you did it.

The real failure is not trying at all.

If you are afraid that a person will judge you for failing, trust me, it is not an opinion that matters. People who are smart and successful don't consider failure a defeat. They know that failure is part of the process. What they will admire about you is your tenacity, your willingness to try again and again, believing it with all of your being, and in the end, you too will look at yourself with courage and pride for being able to go further and finally get where you should be.

You are unique. Your skills, your opinions, and your ideas are personal. Nobody is like you. Nobody can bring your same things to the table; this is what makes you special. Why should you assume that companies might not like you? Why should you think that your CV is not good enough at this point? Who says fashion companies won't like your literature degree? Who says the super famous stylist got an easy start in this industry? Who says you need to have an endless list of skills and experience? Who says, just because you've failed once, twice, or even ten times, fashion is not for you? But above all, who says that when certain skills and requirements are necessary, you cannot acquire them even without a large financial investment?

At this moment I want you to stop telling yourself this lie of not being enough and not deserving the best, which is stopping you. If you keep believing it, you may not even notice it, but your subconscious will decide that you will fail even before you start.

I believe in you, but it is more important that you start believing in yourself if you want to be successful.

You are enough. Go get what's yours.

4

MYTH#1
The Myth of The Dream Job

"I want to work in fashion."

If you are talking to a stranger to the industry and want to give general information about what you would like to do, this explanation of a career goal is fine.

But for yourself this is a statement you should never use.

Saying "I want to work in fashion" means everything and nothing. There are tons of career options in the fashion world. This is why, when you ask me, "I want to work in fashion, what do you advise me to do?" it is difficult to give specific advice because every career in fashion requires different skills and different ways of approaching it.

So point one, let's replace "I want to work in fashion" with:

I want to become a fashion designer.

I want to work as a buyer.

I want to work in communication.

I want to become a stylist.

We will expand on this point in the next chapters.

"My dream is to work for (most of the time, the most important names in the industry come out at this stage) Dior, Gucci, Chanel, Alexander McQueen ..."

I want to invite you to reflect on some things.

Many times we are fascinated by a job title, which we believe is our dream job without even knowing what lies behind that career and what you will actually do when you enter the office every day. But above all, we don't consider whether that job matches our lifestyle, passion, and values.

Becoming the buying manager at Net-a-Porter or the PR director at Dior… they sound like amazing job titles, right?

But based on what information can you say that it represents your dream job? Have you spoken to or seen one of these people at work so that you know what their job is really about? Have you considered whether that career matches your lifestyle, passion, and values?

One day, a student of my online course Break into the Fashion Industry said during our consulting call: "I want to be an editor in chief, but I don't like to write, and I can't write articles."

You do not become editor in chief without having gone through all the various levels, and therefore surely before climbing to the top, you will first need to start as an intern or assistant, and then work as an editor writing or producing articles, before becoming editor in chief. In the end, I helped her realize she was more fascinated by the job title than the actual job, and that she probably watched T*he Devil Wears Prada* too many times.

This idea of a "dream job" is limiting your possibilities.

Since when I started Glam Observer six years ago, I've pushed you to be ambitious and aim for the top. But aiming for the best does not necessarily mean considering only the most prestigious names in the industry and being distracted by the allure of a job title, salary, or a beautiful office. These things might give you short-term satisfaction but they can't compete with the opportunity to find a job that's aligned with your values.

What defines your dream job is not the company name or the title you hold.

The job of your dreams is what you do every single day with passion, the one that on Sunday night you look forward to going to the next morning, the one that stimulates and excites you. You shouldn't choose a job just because it looks good on your resume or LinkedIn profile, or because it sounds glamorous when you talk about it to people.

You don't need a fancy job title to feel satisfied.

You might think that name-dropping a well-known brand/person in the fashion industry will make you look more powerful and proud, but when the conversation ends or when you look at your IG or LinkedIn bio, are you happy? Don't let the no-sense pressure of society make decisions for you. If your friends and acquaintances work at the most established fashion companies, it doesn't mean that if you work at an emerging brand or startup you are less talented. You just have different goals. You are on your own path. You decide if working in a luxury brand is best for you or if you prefer working at your favorite Instagram-born brand. You will be happy and feel satisfied when you do a job that you truly love and not what society, your friends, your school, a TV show, or anything else has imposed on you.

I was working for the top brands of the fashion industry before quitting to focus on Glam Observer. I worked for Kering, YOOX, Net-A-Porter, Alexander McQueen. If you looked at my resume you could have said that I had my dream job. And I thought so for a while. I was working in fashion e-commerce which was my goal when I wanted to enter the fashion industry for the first time. But after one year I realized that even though they were amazing companies that look great on my resume, I was not totally happy and I started feeling that I was on the wrong path.

Even though I liked what I was doing and the brands were absolutely fantastic, that job didn't fit my own lifestyle and passions. I had an entrepreneurial mind already at that time. I wanted to create something and work on my own. Many people said I was brave to leave a job at a top company in a competitive industry. But just because working at the top company is what the society considers cool, or is the dream of your best friends, it doesn't mean it has to be your own dream. I remember in the first months when I quit my job to work at Glam Observer that my friends were working at the top names of the industry. Sometimes I felt uncomfortable during conversations when they were all naming big brands and I said I was working on my business.

Someone looked at me as if I was launching my business because I had no other chance to get into the industry, as if I was settling for that opportunity. I'm glad I never let those opinions discourage me. Yes, it was hard sometimes, but I stayed with my own vision and goal.

It helped me to remind myself what my priorities were.

My friends were working for the top names in the industry, some of them traveled quite often for work, and attended fashion shows and presentations. Of course, going to fashion shows is a dream, it's fantastic, but it's just a moment in time. Do you like your job the other ten months of the year? I was happy for them and I was excited to watch their stories and see they were doing many interesting things, but never to the point where I thought I wanted to quit Glam Observer to do what they are doing.

Don't limit yourself to the career possibilities out there just because you have an idea of a dream job that you have created based on what you see on Instagram, in movies, or online.

We are different and we want different things, luckily! The world is beautiful because it is varied. Imagine if we all wanted to be designers, or all stylists, or work in communication.

Fashion would not exist.

If you see yourself in a luxury brand, that's great!

If you'd rather work at a fashion startup, that's great too!

Do you prefer a sustainable brand?

Working in e-commerce?

A PR agency?

Do you dream of working in a fast fashion brand?

Do you want to work for your favorite fashion magazine? Brilliant!

Any opportunity in fashion is great as long as you've made the decision based on what YOU really want.

The beauty of the fashion industry is that it is made up of so many shades of career options to choose from. We are usually exposed to the most popular careers in the industry, the editor, the designer, the stylist ... but within a fashion company there are so many different professions.

Those who work in finance, lawyers, those who deal with sustainability, production control ...

This creative and fascinating sector works because all of these different figures orchestrate the fashion business. And there is no less important figure than the other, because each of them carries out activities that if no one took care of them would disrupt the rest. From the intern to the CEO, everyone matters.

Understanding what position is ideal for you at the beginning might not be an easy task.

Together with a practical exercise, there are some things I suggest in Break into the Fashion Industry to help students understand what field of fashion is best suited for them.

Here are some of those tips:

1. Consider your passions. Passion is the key ingredient in fashion. Without passion and enthusiasm for your job, you will hardly be successful and able to overcome moments of intense stress. Do you remember the scene in *The Devil Wears Prada* when Emily keeps repeating to herself in a stressful moment: "*I love my job, I love my job, I love my job*"? You will probably say this often too. Only passion will help you to not give up in stressful situations, which are frequent in fashion, especially during peak moments such as fashion week. While this may not be the reality, some people consider working in fashion to be equivalent to saving lives. Fortunately, nobody's life depends on fashion, but maybe your boss doesn't think so, so if nobody's life is physically at risk, your job could be. Passion is the fundamental ingredient that will keep you going and maintain that fundamental curiosity you need to grow. That said, where do you imagine yourself when you think about the fashion industry? Do you work for a fashion magazine? Are you organizing events at a PR agency? Are you a buyer for an online retailer? Are you a stylist who works for a haute couture brand? Do you manage budgets? Are you working within a brand you love that you found on Instagram? Or do you work at companies you've read about in your favorite fashion history books? Write down your career dos and don'ts. These are just some examples:

I DO	I DON'T
Want to work with clothes	Want to work at my desk all day, everyday
Want to work with creative people	Want to travel a lot
Want to learn and grow constantly	Want to work with Excel too much
Want to work at a sustainable brand	Want to work at an agency but only at brands
Want to be part of a start-up	Want to work for a company that doesn't implement diversity
Want to work at a well-established brand	Want to do the same thing every day

Now it's your turn:

I DO	I DON'T

2. While you need to start with your passions to figure out what you'd like to do, the next step is to use the unlimited power of Google, LinkedIn, and Instagram to do your research, gather information, and see if the job you have thought about is actually right for you. There are those who imagine themselves working in PR and then through research, experience, or talking with those who do this job, they realize that they are too introverted or that they do not like having to work in the evening during events and change the career they want to pursue. Search for people who are doing your dream job now, type their name in Google and read their interviews, find them on LinkedIn, read their job description, and contact them to request an informational interview. I have dedicated an entire chapter to the informational interview, but in general, with an informational interview you can contact those who work in fashion to ask questions and understand more about a career, what it means to work in that company, and other informative questions. It's very useful in this research phase to understand what job is made for you but the informational interview has other purposes as well, which we will talk about in the next chapters.

Your research will help you give a clearer idea, but keep in mind that each company has its own structure and organizes departments in different ways and it often happens that the same job title at two different companies have different responsibilities.

For example, the buyer at Gucci could do different things from a buyer at Versace and certainly from that of Harrods.

So, we come to the third point.

3.

Even when you think you have found the right career for you, it is important that you read the job description carefully. Scrolling through job boards is another exercise I recommend to understand which fashion job is right for you. I suggest reading the descriptions of all jobs, even those whose job title doesn't appeal to you. In this way you will have a better understanding of the fashion industry: what are the different careers and figures within a fashion company and what they do. You will see that there are many positions within the fashion business and it is not just about the creative side like design, styling, photography ...

By reading the descriptions of the various job offers in different fashion companies, you may discover a career that you had not considered because you may not have been aware of it. You will also notice what I told you above, that the same title could mean different duties in different companies.

A Fashion Assistant who works in a fashion magazine will do different things than a Fashion Assistant at a brand. Just as the Dior Merchandiser could do different things than the Gucci Merchandiser. So whenever you want to apply for a job, read the job description carefully because every job and company is different.

Your career is an ongoing process. You will change your mind, your passions, and your priorities in a month, or maybe in three years.

After six months of my first internship, I realized that my passions had changed and that even if only one year ago I had moved to Milan with the aim of working in fashion and obtaining a managerial position at a prestigious brand, now I wanted to become the CEO of my company. You may want to go from a luxury brand to working at a startup, from a magazine to a brand, from an agency to a magazine, and from a brand to an agency. You will want to change roles and/ or companies when you feel that you are no longer learning new things, when you feel you are not challenging yourself enough, when you don't like your team, or so on. In fashion, people change jobs on average every 2-3 years!

The older generation of people who started their careers and ended it at the same company doing the same job no longer exists.
What you think is your dream job today probably won't be in a year. You will ask yourself many times in your career path what you want to do and what you are good at. Understanding what your path is not an exercise that you will do only now when you are at the beginning of your career. That's why it's important to not stress yourself out too much thinking about having to choose a career that you will enjoy and that will suit you even in five, ten, or fifteen years.

They ask us to make important decisions when we are still at the beginning of our lives. Choosing a university path or a first job is like trying to predict what we will enjoy for the rest of our lives. But there are few people who at age forty do the job they thought they'd do at age eighteen and is related to what they studied. Perhaps only doctors fall into this category. You have no idea how many people who have studied law did not become lawyers, or studied engineering and did not become engineers (me, for example).

That's why some prefer to choose something more generic that is easily adaptable with a little bit of everything. A degree in economics or communications, for example. In any case, we have seen that what you have studied will not affect your future choices and neither will the first job you choose. You can change and change again.

What if you like more than one fashion career?

In recent consultations with the students of Break into the Fashion Industry and The Freelance Fashion Writer Boss, what has come up quite often is having to decide between two passions and two different career options. The question is always something like: "I like [fashion career 1] and [fashion career 2] , how do I choose one?"

I always respond like this: "Mix them up."

Today, with many digital careers and the speed of our society, I don't think that any of us should be tied to a single job title anymore if you do have more than one passion. And to be honest, the thought of you having to give up one dream kills me. I'll never be the person telling you that you can't do anything. Because I'm confident that you can achieve whatever you want in life if you believe in yourself and are ready to do the work. I'm not saying it's going to be easy, but you know the best things in life are never easy, especially having more than one job.

Today you can see more and more people who have more than one job title that describes them in their Instagram bio and LinkedIn profile. They are not just stylists, pr, fashion designers, editors: they are stylists and freelance writers, they are fashion directors and consultants, they are publicists and brand founders...

Of course, there are still people who love their one job and are happy with it and want to do it for the rest of their life without the need for something more, but there are also many people who have multiple passions and so who are multihyphenates.

To be able to pursue two career options at the same time, you have to be very organized, productive, and also, of course, be willing to have less free time. If you do have a full-time job and want to launch your fashion brand or write fashion articles on the side, you'll probably do it in the evenings and during the weekend, therefore having a packed schedule every day of the week.

Of course, it's impossible to have two full-time jobs at the same time as you can imagine, so if you have more than one passion, one of them should be done remotely, as a freelancer and/or with flexible hours. If you can find both jobs with flexible hours than this is a jackpot as you can organize your time as you prefer. In general, unless both career options are freelance jobs or you work on your own, one of the two jobs involves working with other people and so you are fixed to the working hours of others.

Some career options that are more likely to combine with another full-time job, because doable as a freelancer, are:

writing
consulting (you can consult about PR, styling, marketing, art direction, business, social media ... in general something you are specialized in)
starting your own blog, podcast, or brand
photography

that you can combine with a full-time job in buying, marketing, merchandising, pr, styling, finance, fashion design.

For example, stylists who might have more fixed hours when working with photographers, makeup artists, and models for photo shoots, if they also want to write for fashion publications, they do so in the evenings, during the weekend, lunch break, or anytime they have a couple of hours in between shoots. Same goes for buyers, publicists, those who work in marketing, or fashion designers who have a 9-5 job: to pursue a second career, whether it is launching a fashion label, consulting, writing, or starting a blog ... they have to run it on the side. Another option, less common than the previous one, is to have two part-time jobs. So you could be working 2-3 days at one job and the rest of the week at your second job or work in the morning at one job and in the afternoon at another.

This option is less common as in fashion it is difficult to find part-time jobs that are not sales assistant jobs or internships. Most of the junior, mid-level, and senior corporate jobs require your presence in the office full-time, so unless you are working as a freelancer/consultant it is more difficult.

Combining more than one job is something you can explore at the beginning of your career when you want to understand what is made for you or even later when you just want to follow two different passions or become a consultant after years in the corporate world.

Whatever you choose, do it considering your current passions. If they happen to stay the same, fine, but if you want to totally shake up your path, that's okay too! You can do it. I know many people who studied law and today work as buyers. What you choose today does not determine what your whole life will be; the important thing is to choose for yourself.

You are the only one who defines what your dream job is.

5

MYTH#2
Those who work in fashion wear designer clothes everyday

Working in fashion does not automatically mean wearing only designer clothes, having a new look each day to go to the office, or changing the way one dresses.

The fact that those who work in fashion wear expensive clothes and shoes every day is another myth of this industry. I invite you to go to Instagram and see the stories of those who work in fashion and their elevator selfies (The Hearst Group has a personalized hashtag *#hearstelevatorselfie)* to see what those who work in fashion wear every day. You will notice that they almost certainly dress like you already do every day.

The opening scene of *The Devil Wears Prada* which shows

different women getting ready in the morning, each carefully chosen clothes and heels, remains a classic. We would all like the experience of getting dressed in the morning to be as fabulous as that, but in reality, (although the mornings after I watch that movie I am more motivated to dress like that), most people dress in a hurry as they rush off to work. Since you'll likely be away from home all day you will probably wear heels in moderation, preferring comfortable shoes, sneakers, loafers, or flat sandals in summer and boots in winter. There will be exceptions and those days when you feel like putting in that extra effort, but in most cases you will prefer to feel comfortable rather than being in uncomfortable clothes or shoes for ten hours or more. Especially if your job involves going from one part of the city to another and running errands.

The Devil Wears Prada has been very influential on young people who want to enter the fashion world and they often consider it as a reference model to understand how the industry works. But what you see in that movie doesn't quite represent the reality. When Miranda says to Andy that she took a chance hiring the "smart fat girl," that scene is wrong for various reasons. First of all, Andy is far from being overweight, secondly, people who work in fashion come in all sizes, and, above all, your weight does not affect your career success!

Some of you have asked me if your appearance, the way you dress, and your weight are important for getting a job in fashion.

Unless you want to work as a model where you will be asked for your measurements (luckily fashion companies are starting to diversify and make space for models of different shapes), your weight and your height don't matter if you want to work as a buyer, merchandiser, stylist, designer, photographer... or any other job.

Of course this is an industry that puts more pressure on one's appearance than any other.

There are people who will pay attention to the way you dress more than in any other industry. They will notice what you wear especially when the ability to perfectly match clothes is part of your job, in the case of a stylist. Even in this case, many famous stylists, however, wear basic pieces and then create amazing looks of all kinds on their clients or for editorials. In fact, choosing basic garments is always the right choice when you don't know what to wear or don't feel comfortable with other looks.

Just because people will look at the way you are dressed doesn't mean you have to wear whimsical pieces or the latest designer releases, or need to be constantly changing your look.

Matching clothes is an art, an innate skill that people have.

Dressing well is not a necessary prerequisite to get the job. It's true that some companies put more pressure on this and someone might look at you as snobbily as Miranda looked at Andy (it's impossible not to refer to *The Devil wears Prada*) but as we said in the previous chapter, you choose what conditions matter when deciding where to work. If you don't feel like working at a company where they make you feel out of place for what you wear, change companies or weigh the options: if it's the job you like, maybe it's worth making an extra effort? Do what feels right for you. You have to find compromises with and for yourself.

In fashion, you are often exposed to people who dress perfectly every day, but you don't have to dress like Anna Dello Russo if it's not your style or you might get the opposite effect. Looking at colleagues, stylists, and models who are always impeccable and wear amazing looks should be inspiring but in the end, you have to dress like yourself if you want to avoid feeling out of place and thinking all day about what you are wearing rather than your job.

Have you ever noticed how creative directors are dressed when they come out to get the well-deserved applause at the end of each fashion show? They always wear basic garments and many have their own uniform that they always repeat: Anna Wintour is known for always wearing a floral dress and her choker necklaces along with her black Chanel sunglasses, Miuccia Prada wears a sweater and long skirt. Some do it as a matter of practicality and avoid taking too long to get dressed in the morning, but in general once you have found the look that suits you and with which you feel comfortable but also confident, there is nothing wrong with replicating it.

During my first internship I had my first experience with this world. I was the youngest in the office, but some of my colleagues were just a little older than me so it was easy to compare. They frequently shopped online, got their nails done every week, took yoga classes, weekend trips ... When you're an intern, it's already a lot if you're getting paid, and when you're lucky, you can barely cover the necessary expenses such as rent and food. Luckily I have never been an envious person; even when I was doing my internship and looking at my colleagues, I knew I was just starting out so it was normal for them to have other lifestyles and other salaries. I have never made a comparison in this sense. In fact, I loved the moment when the packages arrived at the office and we opened them together. But I know some people who, exposed to all of this, allowed themselves to be tempted and bought clothes or accessories when they could not afford them, just to fit in, and it didn't end well.

In fashion, you generally get discounts on the brand's products you work for that can range from 20% up to 50% and you also have access to exclusive sales periods for employees where you can get great deals. It is easy to be tempted on these occasions, but when I was an intern it was pretty much my entire salary even after the discount, so I limited myself to buying a pair of Adidas x Stella McCartney sneakers that to be honest, I didn't really need. I let myself be taken by the thrill of wanting to feel part of that occasion in which everyone was buying and I bought what I could without thinking about it. Fortunately,

I didn't get carried away to the point of spending my entire salary on one bag.

If you want to work in fashion, I'm sure you also have a penchant for designer shoes, bags, and clothes, but remember to stay true to yourself. You have to make your own experiences according to what's best for you and your circumstances at the time. Your day will come too. It's normal for you to be on a different timeline than those around you. You don't have to conform to everyone around you and there is no need to spend all of your salary on designer clothes. In the meantime, you can do your own manicure at home, go for a run outdoors, or watch videos on YouTube if you want to do yoga. You can also be professional and stylish by purchasing affordable brands on Amazon, Asos, Uniqlo, or Zalando. Look at sites like Vestiare Collective or vintage shops to find some interesting gems and, when your time comes, if you want, you can buy the latest piece by your favorite designer.

It's great to reuse your clothes again on many different occasions and events even in fashion, especially now that everyone is interested in sustainability. Your black dress that you already wore for three events will also be appreciated for future ones. Celebrities do it, you can too!

It's important to care about your image, and think about what to wear because you still work in fashion, but this doesn't mean having to overdo it or spend all of your salary on clothes.

The way you dress and look makes you feel more confident but only as long as what you wear represents you. Just because a look is good on someone doesn't mean it looks good or fits your style. Over time, I realized that rather than wanting to change my body to get into a dress that doesn't fit me, I should choose something that enhances my body. I tried some looks I had seen on Instagram and I discovered that if that influencer looked great in that dress, it didn't suit me at all. Everyone has their own body type and you shouldn't try to adapt at all costs to what you see online or on others or you'll end up not liking yourself and triggering unhealthy mental conditions.

Working in an industry where you are constantly exposed to beautiful models and magazine covers featuring girls that are too skinny can make you question your body shape and lose some of the confidence you had in your appearance.

If you were someone else who didn't want to work in fashion, I'd suggest you stop consuming magazines or looking at models' Instagram profiles if they get you down. When you work in fashion you can't avoid looking at beautiful models. However, leaner doesn't mean more success, more career opportunities, and better clothes! Your weight doesn't define you. And above all, are we really still at the point where we compare ourselves with models or feel like we have to conform to a popular influencer? Come on.

So find the look that makes you feel confident. For example, a blazer is enough for me to immediately feel more "girlboss." While I love my Uniqlo blue merino wool sweater for everyday office looks and I like to have a polished look: a nude nail polish, eyebrows in place, concealer to cover dark circles, a touch of mascara and blush, and my favorite Charlotte Tilbury Pillow Talk pencil, and I immediately feel ready and above all, myself.

6

MYTH#3
It's All About Clothes, Parties, And Creativity

Fashion is a giant ecosystem and one of the biggest industries in the world, generating \$2.5 trillion in global annual revenues.[1] In 2019 the fashion industry contributed £35 billion to the British economy and employed 890,000 people,[2] 495,000 in Italy,[3] and more than 1.8 million people in the United States,[4] with 28,300 jobs specifically in fashion design. [5]

The fashion industry is well known for the clothes, the creativity, and the shows/events, but it's much more than that.
Those who work inside the industry know that the shoes, clothes, accessories, and bags are the result of the work of thousands of people and that events and parties are part of the marketing strategy.

Famous reality fashion programs such as *Project Runway*, *Next in Fashion*, and *Making the Cut* show the role of the fashion designer exclusively, and the designer is usually the first career associated with fashion. Many approach this world convinced that they want to design clothes, then go deeper to discover an entire fascinating world that revolves around the fashion industry, eventually changing their minds about what career to pursue.

Behind a fashion brand there are many layers and so many professions that, even if I have already included a chapter focused only on fashion careers, it is still impossible to list them all.

People look at a dress in a store without thinking about the number of people involved in the production and marketing of that single garment, and the life cycle of the raw materials used for textile production, which began in fields all over the world. Although it may seem that it is an industry based on the designer's creativity, in reality all the choices in fashion are based on numbers: how did previous sales go? This dress has sold more than that dress, why? What are the trends of the market? How are the competitors doing? How much was spent on marketing? What was the ROI?

In the end, fashion companies have to make ends meet, it's not enough to produce the best dress if it doesn't sell. That's why working in fashion does not only mean producing and designing beautiful clothes and selling them in stores; just like working at fashion magazines doesn't mean just writing articles and shooting editorials—it is so much more.

If it's true that, unlike other industries, you have to deal mainly with clothes, it does not mean that those who work in fashion spend all day working with them. Given the diversity and depth of the roles in a fashion company, there are those who never touch clothes with their hands! Where I worked for example, I happened to see clothes only a couple of times a year when I went to the showroom.

When I first entered the industry, I didn't expect to see everyone who works in fashion spend hours and hours on Excel and lots of emails. Not only those who work in finance, buying, merchandising, and communication, but even stylists use Excel to organize the clothes they receive and return for photo shoots.

The fashion industry is often thought of as superficial and fun, a perfect and glamorous world where everything seems to flow smoothly and the worst that can happen is that a dress is not ready to hit the runway (which by the way, in fashion is serious). In reality, due to its characteristics and working rhythms, fashion is one of the industries, together with that of technology, in which workers suffer the most from stress, and designers have even suffered from mental problems due to stress.

The work days are long, and often go beyond normal working hours. It is rare that those who work in fashion manage to leave the office at 6 p.m., and they often work on weekends, especially during times such as fashion week. And in some cases, 24/7 availability is required, blurring the line between personal and working life.

Fashion can be a serious business, and companies don't make fashion just for the sake of it. There are many economic, social, and cultural factors that influence the decisions of a fashion company.

To quote Coco Chanel:

Fashion is not something that exists in dresses only. Fashion is in the sky, in the street, fashion has to do with ideas, the way we live, what is happening.

Think of the slogan "We should all be feminist," from the title of the book by Nigerian writer Chimamanda Ngozi Adichie, that Maria Grazia Chiuri, the first female artistic director of Dior, adopted on a t-shirt for her debut Spring Summer 2017 collection presented in September 2016.

Or the issue of sustainability that companies have to face every day. According to the Ellen MacArthur Foundation, the global fashion industry produces about 53 million tonnes of fiber every year. More than 70% of that ends up in landfills or on bonfires. Less than 1% is reused to make new clothes.

The textile sector still accounts for 6% of global greenhouse gas emissions and 10 to 20% of pesticide use. Washes, solvents, and dyes used in manufacturing are responsible for one-fifth of industrial water pollution and fashion accounts for 20 to 35% of microplastic in the ocean[6]. On 26 August 2019, François-Henri Pinault, President and CEO of Kering the luxury group to which brands such as Gucci, Saint Laurent, Balenciaga, Bottega Veneta, Alexander McQueen and others belong, proposed a solution at the heads of state meeting at the G7 summit in Biarritz. Luxury and fast fashion brands discussed what they could do to protect the environment by signing the Fashion Pact. Thirty-two leading companies, including Nike, Chanel, Prada, H&M, and Calzedonia Group, signed the pact with the intention of protecting the oceans by sustainably sourcing raw materials in an effort to reduce chemicals in water supplies and oceans, focus on biodiversity and climate change, achieve zero carbon emissions by 2050, eliminate single-use plastics in B2B and D2C, and move to 100% renewable energy by 2030.

Some brands, such as H&M, Levi's, and Patagonia, are trying to reduce waste and the problem of fabric disposal, with programs to take back clothes that consumers no longer wear. The fabrics of these clothes are converted into fashion and other industries' products. So, rather than throwing old clothes away like other waste and entrusting them to inappropriate disposal processes that would pollute, it's right to hand them over to the stores of these brands that promote these ecological initiatives (H&M provides even a 15% discount on the next purchase to those who deliver used clothes to their stores!).

Consumers' attention to the impact of the fashion industry on the environment has contributed to the increasing popularity of secondhand clothing, giving new life to garments that are no longer worn by reselling them, and in turn buying secondhand clothes from apps and websites such as Depop and Vestiaire Collective.

In October 2020, Levi's announced the creation of a buy-back and resale program called Levi's SecondHand, which will allow customers to buy pre-owned Levi's pieces directly from the brand for prices ranging from $30 to $100.

"Buying a used pair of Levi's through SecondHand saves approximately 80% of the $CO2$ emissions and 700 grams of waste compared to buying a new pair of Levi's," according to Levi's CMO Jennifer Sey.

In a similar announcement, Gucci is now partnering with The RealReal, which will feature a new dedicated Gucci e-commerce site for secondhand pieces from consignors and from the brand itself. Gucci joins a growing number of brands that are taking control of their own resale markets: Stella McCartney paved the way as the first luxury brand to partner with The RealReal in 2017, and Burberry followed in 2019.

Fashion responds to social problems.

Let's think about how George Floyd's death in May 2020 also had repercussions on the fashion industry which was accused of still having many weaknesses in terms of diversity within corporate offices (a 2019 report on Inclusion & Diversity in the American Fashion Industry revealed that only 56% of respondents said they had taken a professional course or seminar related to inclusion and diversity[7]). Only 3% of the members of the Council of Fashion Designers of America are black and at New York Fashion Week Fall/Winter 2019, only 10% of the designers were black[8]. It is the same in Italy, where Stella Jean is the only black designer who is a member of Camera Moda.

In various situations the fashion industry has been called into question for racism both in advertising campaigns and a lack of diversity within companies. Think about Gucci's "blackface" sweater, for example, which prompted the brand to invest $10 million in a program that aims to encourage internal diversity and inclusion.

The goal of this chapter is not just to inform you about the dynamics of the fashion industry and to ask you to question the various issues that surround it, but to show you that, although clothes are the product around which everything revolves, there is much more behind it.

I also wrote this chapter because you represent the future of the fashion industry, so it is important that you support these important issues in the companies where you will work and perhaps, why not, consider a career that focuses on sustainability and diversity. Fashion is influenced by everything that happens in the world, both on a creative level and in managerial decisions. It is not enough to know only who the fashion designers are, to have good style, and know what new trends have been forecast, it is also necessary to inquire about culture, economy, communication, and technology ... if you want to work in this industry.

1-6. State of fashion 2020, McKinsey, April 7 2020 https://www.mckinsey.com/industries/retail/our-insights/its-time-to-rewire-the-fashion-system-state-of-fashion-coronavirus-update

2. British Fashion Council Annual Report 2019-2020, British Fashion Council https://www.britishfashioncouncil.co.uk/uploads/files/1/BFC%20Annual%20Report%202019-20.pdf

3. Number of employees in the textile and clothing industry in Italy 2014-2019, Statista, August 5 2020 https://www.statista.com/statistics/1004004/number-of-employees-in-the-textile-and-clothing-industry/

4. The Economic Impact of the Fashion Industry, Joint Economic Committee Democrats, February 22 2019 https://www.jec.senate.gov/public/index.cfm/democrats/reports?ID=449944BB-EF17-42CC-B9EF-15E8AC01FCB8

5 Occupational Outlook Handbook > Arts and Design >Fashion Designers, U.S. BUREAU OF LABOR STATISTICS, September 1 2020 https://www.bls.gov/ooh/arts-and-design/fashion-designers.html

7 Inclusion & Diversity in the American Fashion Industry, January 2019 https://cfda.imgix.net/2019/01/CFDA-PVH_Insider-Outsider_Final_01-2019.pdf

8. Why these Gucci clothes are racist, Business Insider, February 27 2019 https://www.businessinsider.com/why-gucci-clothes-racist-blackface-sambo-2019-2?IR=T

PART II

Habits to adopt for a successful fashion career

7

HOW TO SET YOUR FASHION CAREER GOALS

As I said in the introduction, the aim of this book is to guide you to turn your dream of a fashion career into reality. In order to do so, it's important to replace the word "dream" with the word "goal."

My dream is to get a job in fashion
becomes
My goal is to get a job in fashion.

Can you see how immediately everything changes when we use the word goal? In your mind, what was an abstract dream immediately seems more practical, more real. When your mind knows that you have a goal, it's going to act in your favor and will prioritize this goal because it knows you have a purpose to achieve. If you keep saying that this is your dream, your mind will treat it just like a fantasy, something to leave to your imagination, something that doesn't require action. But taking action is the only thing that will make everything happen.

Even though in this book we are going to focus on your fashion career goals, it's important that you set goals for whatever you want to achieve in your life.

At this time your goal could be to land your first internship, then it might be to turn an internship into a full-time job, then to get a promotion, to work on a project you're passionate about, to launch your fashion brand, to go to work with your favorite brands, and on and on. You should always have a new goal after you have achieved one. If you don't set goals, days, weeks, and months will pass and it's like life is living you instead of the other way around. You need to take charge of your life and your career.

Especially in times of uncertainty, like with the recent pandemic that changed the world, having a purpose is super important to stay motivated and inspired even during hard times.

Your goals should be the reason why you wake up energized every day, hungry to conquer whatever you want in life.

So how do you set your fashion career goals?

The way you set your goals will make a difference in your results. If you have ever felt like you were working hard but not getting results, it's either because you started acting without a plan in place, or because you didn't do it the correct way.

1. Set <u>specific</u> goals

8 of 10 emails I get say:

"I studied literature, how can I get a job in fashion?"
"I'm about to graduate in marketing/design/communication/styling... how do I get a job in fashion?"
"I want to work at Gucci/Jacquemus/ Dior/Chanel... how can I do this?"
Saying you want to get a job in fashion or just naming a brand means everything and nothing as we said in "The Myth of the Dream job" chapter.

The fashion industry is made up of many career possibilities and for each career, there are different pathways.

If you want to get a job as a designer, the first step I'd suggest is to build your portfolio, even before applying. If you want to become a buyer I'd suggest looking for buying internships. If you want to become a stylist, reach out to stylists and ask if you can assist them.

As you can see, there are different paths for each career option. If you want to achieve your goal of getting into the fashion industry and you need to set a series of actions to take, you first need to be specific with your goal or you won't know what steps to take. Saying *I want to get a job in fashion* is too generic and it doesn't allow you to understand how to achieve it.

So instead of saying:

"I want to get a job in fashion"
be specific:
"I want to get a job in Fashion PR at a luxury company"
or
 "I want to get a job as a buyer in New York"
These are specific goals.

If you know that you want to get a job in fashion PR at a luxury company, you are narrowing the circle of possibilities. So you can filter the jobs in your search phase by looking at only communication jobs at luxury brands.

If you want to become a buyer in New York, you can filter the jobs to New York City only and search using the keyword "buyer."

Can you see how being specific with your goal can immediately give you more clarity on what steps to take?

OK, let's try it together.

Stop for a minute and think about your fashion dream.

Where do you see yourself working?

Do you work at a fashion magazine? Do you write for the magazine or are you a stylist?

Do you work at a fashion brand? Are you a buyer, are you a designer, are you working in marketing?

Do you work at a PR or modeling agency?

Do you work in a store or in a showroom?

Who are the people you are working with?

Are you on a photo shoot set? Are you traveling and discovering new collections and brands? Are you producing clothes?

Are you working in Milan, London, Paris, New York, Munich, Florence, Berlin? Are you working remotely?

Are you working at a luxury brand/fast fashion/ online retailer/ tech company?

Are you working for an established brand or a startup?

Take five minutes and close your eyes. Visualize yourself where you want to be. Dream big. Sleep on it or take a week to think about this. It's important.

But don't stress yourself too much about having to decide now what you are going to do for the rest of your life.

Focus on what you want now.

In fashion, people change jobs and companies on average every three years. Your first job will likely not be the one you have for the rest of your life. The older generation of people who stayed at the same company and did the same job throughout their entire career doesn't exist anymore.

Today people have multiple jobs at the same time. You can be a designer and write for fashion magazines on the side as a freelancer. You can work as a stylist and also be an editor. You can work in PR and as a photographer as well. You can be an art director and an influencer. If you have multiple passions, you can mix them up.

So focus on what you like now. Consider your passions and remember what we have said in the previous chapter: you are enough, so dream big and don't limit your dreams because you think you can't make it with what you have now. Don't say to me, and to yourself mostly, that you might prefer to work at a local brand if you dream about working in fashion houses such as Dior, Chanel, and Gucci, just because you think they are too out of reach for you.

Dream big in this phase.

I had a consultation with a student one day and she was about to apply for a visual merchandising role. She knew she wanted to work in communication, so I asked her why was she applying for a visual merchandising job if it was not bringing her closer to her end goal?

I asked: "Why do you want to waste precious time of your life getting a job in visual merchandising when you can do a PR internship and be already one step closer to your dream of working in communication?"

She said she was applying to the visual merchandising job just because it seemed easier to get because it didn't require lots of experience.

This is a big mistake.

The truth was that she didn't have her goal in mind, because as soon as I said that she could have interned in PR, she immediately went back on track. That choice was not helping her career. If you already have a clear idea of what career path to take, you should take the steps to get closer to it.

Do you really want to waste six months of your life doing an internship that you don't need to do and doesn't give you the skills that you need, then have to find another internship in your field of choice because your dream job needs someone with relevant experience?

Setting goals helps you to not lose focus on what you want to achieve and motivates you to take the actions that will get you there.

2. Write down your goal

Once you have your goal in mind, write it down. Successful people rely on this practice and many books, articles, and research studies have proven that those who write down their goals are more likely to achieve them. So once you have visualized it in your mind, write your goal down.

Write it here, write it on your smartphone notes, write it on a Post-it, write it in a journal. Write it as if it has already become a reality. So if your goal is to work at a **PR** firm in Milan write:

I'm working at a **PR** firm in Milan.

Write it where you can see it every single day. I'd love for you to say that you'll carry this book with you forever and wherever you go but that's probably not realistic, so make sure to write your goal in your iPhone notes or in your agenda.

3. Think about 5 steps to achieve your goal

Awesome, now that you have your goal written on top of that Post-it or in a notebook, you need to think about the steps to take to get closer to where you want to go.

Writing down a plan helps you to understand exactly what you need to do, and the steps you need to take. Do you remember when I said that I'm a practical and pragmatic person? That I need to follow steps to reach my goals?

Well, now we will do just that by establishing the various steps to achieve your career goal.

Let's say that the goal you wrote down is: I write for fashion magazines.

Well, if you think about activities that will get you closer to your goal, your plan might include writing a couple of articles to send, along with your CV and cover letter, when you apply. Or starting a blog to have something to show to the editor. Or going to fashion panels where your favorite editors speak, meeting them in person, and asking for their email address so that you can send over your work. Your plan could also include finding your favorite editors on LinkedIn and connecting with them by asking for an informational interview.

If you want to work in PR and you've just graduated, one of the actions of your plan is to get a PR internship and then turn a PR internship into a full-time job.

Take again that notebook page or iPhone note where you wrote down your goal, and write down at least five things you can think of that will help you get closer to your ultimate goal.

These are some examples of activities you should write down:

Go to networking events

Book a flight to go to the job interview

Find an apartment and work in a new city

Find my dream job online

Write my CV and a cover letter

Find the recruiter's email

Apply for jobs

Connect with people working at the company you are applying for on LinkedIn

Having a plan written down with the actions you need to take will help you get to your end goal. If you have your plan of actions written down, you won't lose the focus and you won't end up making decisions or taking actions that are unrelated to your end goals such as applying for an internship that is completely unrelated to your dream job.

Ok, now that you have a list of actions, read them over again. Out of the five actions, there is only one that is absolutely necessary to start with. Going to networking events is important, but it's not the first and absolutely necessary step to get a job in fashion. Find out which is the one thing you absolutely need to start with. Probably it will be to start by finding a job? Or focusing on your CV and portfolio?

Now that you know where you need to start from, think about what resources you already have and those you need to get.

Do you need to set up a LinkedIn profile? Do you need to refresh your CV? Do you need to take an online course to grow your skills? Do you need to find the email address of the person you'd like to cold email for a job?

Let's assume you will start with your CV. Where do you begin when creating a CV? Will you use a template? Will you design and write it yourself? Once you have your starting point, just do it.Now that you have your CV ready, what is the next step on that list? Looking for jobs or internships online? Listing your favorite brands so that you can email them about a possible internship?

After establishing the action to start with to achieve your goal, assign an order to all the others on the list.

I have prepared an example of steps for three careers, head over to www.glamobserver.com/book to download it for free.

When you have assigned an order to all the steps, just do everything you need, step-by-step, to reach your end goal.

Keep your destination in mind, and don't forget that mistakes are a huge learning opportunity. You can always change and try a new approach if something is not working.

Write down your steps here and on that same page, post-it, iPhone notes where you wrote your goal:

MY FASHION CAREER GOAL:

_____

ACTIONS

1.
2.
3.
4.
5.

4. Fail, adjust, and try again!

If you are not getting responses when you apply for jobs, your problem could be your CV, your cover letter, your portfolio, the type of jobs you are applying for, or your approach to getting a job. Are you only applying online? Are you only applying for a few jobs each month?

You might need to tweak something in your strategy if you don't see results; maybe you haven't been consistent enough, or maybe you left that list of steps on the piece of paper without taking action?

I got a message from a girl once who asked me: "Are there people that take your course and still don't find a job?"

Well, in the course I teach you strategies, I give you CV, cover letter, and email templates and resources to use, but if you don't actually put your own work into it, if you don't act, then you won't see results. Watching the lessons or reading this book won't take you anywhere if you don't apply the strategies consistently. This is for everything in life. It's not enough to get a gym membership or hire a personal trainer. If you want to get fit you need to put in effort, you need to work out every single day. It is not enough to enroll in a fashion school to get a job, you must be proactive in the job search, making the most out of the opportunities through your school and learning how to apply in a way that makes you stand out among all the others.

If you don't work hard, if you're not proactive, then you won't get what you want. The tools and the resources we find help us to continue on this journey of reaching for our goals, but you have to do the work, learn from your failures, adjust, and try again.

5. Be consistent

Overnight success doesn't exist.

You get results from the actions you take consistently, not from something you do once or a few times.

Once you have the list of actions to take, you can't just do the things on your list once and hope to see results. We have already said that hope is not a strategy.
You need to show up and do the things on your list every day, step-by-step until you reach your end goal.
Being consistent is very important for achieving what you want in life. I have dedicated an entire chapter to consistency and how to form good habits, which we will see in a bit.

Okay, so to recap, we have just said that in order to achieve a goal:

1. It must be specific
2. Write it down

3. Think about five actions needed to reach it and identify the first absolutely necessary step to get started with

4. Assign an order to all the other steps

4. Act and possibly make corrections if necessary

5. Be consistent

Setting your goals correctly is the first step towards achieving them.

The fact that you have transformed what was a dream into a goal to be achieved and written it down is already a giant step towards its realization. Your mind now sees what was a dream as much more concrete and achievable. Identifying the goal is the fundamental step to begin with, but there are many practices that must be implemented in order to get to the finish line.

From today on, your goal will no longer be one of many on the list of New Year's resolutions that we write on January 1st and forget about it ten days later. From today you will be determined to want to achieve what you wrote in that notebook and you will not stop until you have achieved it. From today you are the strongest and most determined person you know. From today you firmly believe that your dream will soon come true because you have a plan.

In this second part of the book we will focus on habits and mindsets to adopt to make sure that everything converts to your result.

Let's begin.

8

CAREER MOOD BOARD, MOTIVATIONAL ALARMS, AND SHOPPING REWARDS

I have to admit, until a few years ago, I was one of those people who makes a list of resolutions on January 1st, and every year it's almost always the same.

In the last two years, however, my list for the new year has been different from the previous one. Not because I've changed my mind about what I want, but because over the past twelve months I managed to check most things off my list, both personal and professional.

At a certain point I realized that it made no sense to make that list every year if nothing, or almost nothing, had changed. Perhaps I had achieved some other goals that year, but if that was the case, it's because they just happened. I no longer wanted to leave things only to chance. If you plan to go to New York but you find an amazing airfare deal to London, you take it, or if you had the goal of working at *Vogue* and *Harper's Bazaar* calls, you respond. When these unexpected things happen, you have to be open to welcoming them; planning does not mean giving up on everything else that is not on the list regardless. I decided I wanted to take control of my life by taking action towards what I had established as my priorities and goals while still being open to the unexpected (after all, I love surprises).

As much as we would like, it is impossible to always stay highly motivated if we don't stimulate our mind on a daily basis.
We are all super busy, we have a thousand things to think about, it is easy to lose focus. So, writing down your goals and being determined is not enough. Our mind needs some assistance. I decided to change my mindset in order to stay focused. In this chapter, I want to share with you four practices that have made a huge difference in achieving results and have allowed me to take that giant step between saying and doing.

1. Write down your goals every single day

I am a stylist based in Los Angeles who dresses celebrities.
I am the buyer of a department store.
I am a designer and I have my own fashion brand.
I am a web merchandiser of a luxury e-commerce.

Over the past year I've started writing my goals every single day, first thing in the morning.

Now you are probably thinking that writing down goals every single morning sounds crazy, but trust me it will help you immensely in maintaining focus, motivation, and setting the right mindset for each new day. Take a diary and use it just to write down your goals each morning. You can also do this while you're still in bed if you want.

Writing down your goals and not taking action obviously won't change your life, but doing this simple task in the morning will motivate you and remind you every single day to take action. Your unconscious will work and act for you! Writing down your goals instead of leaving them just in your mind doubles the chance of achieving them. Here we want to increase this possibility even more, by writing them not just once, but every single day.

I want to give you an example of how this concept of writing goals every day (that might sound crazy) actually works.

Something amazing happened in March 2020. I was included in the Under 30 list for *Forbes Italy*, the famous annual list of influential people. I only found out about it the day before the issue was released on newsstands and online, and it was a (positive) shock for me. I was included in the Education section for my work with Glam Observer, guiding those who want to work in fashion. Would you believe me if I told you that every morning starting on January 1, 2020, I had written among my goals: *I'm on the Forbes Under 30 list?*

I have admired the people on that list for years, and one of my resolutions for 2020 was to see my name among all the other entrepreneurs! I wanted to make my dream a reality this time. So I knew I had to go from a dream to a goal. I started writing it every day as one of my goals, and then it happened (thanks Roberta Maddalena for selecting me and believing in me!)

There is something powerful about writing down your goals and visualizing yourself doing what you love. You start attracting all the things that will make it happen and if you do it every day imagine how much you can attract! My story is just one example. If I did it, you can too! Another goal for 2020 was to publish a book, and guess what? Having it on my list and writing it as a goal every day prompted me to finally start writing the book. Of course, just writing to become a best-selling author doesn't make it happen, but it gave me inspiration and motivation, and I think I started attracting all the things I needed to publish it. Every day writing that goal reminded me that I had to do something to reach it: the first day I wrote down the content outline, the following day I wrote that goal again, which motivated me to do some research, the next day I began writing the first words of the book, etc...

While this is a career book, it doesn't mean your goals need to be only professional. I write about ten goals, a mix of personal and professional. I think the right focus and motivation allows you to have that perfect balance of career and personal life.

I know that there are many people who say that you cannot have a successful career and an equally fantastic private life, especially if you are a woman. But I think that you can get everything you want and find the right compromises without having to give up one or the other. This practice helps me stay focused both on my personal and professional life.

So, from today on, write down your goals every morning:
I am a buyer who travels between Milan, Paris, London, and New York
Visit Marrakech
Buy a house
Turn my internship into a job
Get a raise
…
Don't wait for the following year but expand your list as soon as you reach your goals (we are ambitious here!)

2. The Inspirational Career Mood Board

One day, while watching *The Intern*, one of my favorite movies, I realized how much more motivated I am the day after I watch it. Jules Ostin (played by Anne Hathaway) is an entrepreneur who has built her own fashion company (if you haven't watched that movie yet, do it now, you'll love Robert De Niro as a 70-year-old intern) and I saw myself in her with Glam Observer: starting from scratch and creating a successful company with a team of hundreds of people (I don't have a team of hundreds of people yet but hope to soon and that's where the motivation comes in!). When I wanted to get my job in fashion, I had the same feelings whenever I watched *The Devil wears Prada*.

Then I realized...

Images motivate me enormously. And so I started thinking about a way to give my mind this inspirational dose daily.

Of course, I can't watch that movie every day, but I can look at images every day. I started thinking about my goals and associated an image with each of them, then created a collage and set it as the background for my desktop and smartphone. Looking at it every day pushes me, even unconsciously, to take action!

Let's focus again on your fashion career goal. Choose images that inspire you in relation to it: the office of your favorite company, a photo of an editor, stylist, or anyone who you admire who has your dream job...

Collect the images, create a mood board, and use it as the background of your smartphone and desktop and, if you want, print it and hang it where you can see it every day. If your mind visualizes the goal, it will begin to act together with you and lead you to success.

I have prepared a couple of moad boards that you can download for free and use for your desktop or smarphone, visit www. glamobserver.com/book

Looking at these pictures and visualizing your goal will inspire you enormously and give you the energy and motivation you need to take action every day and make your dream a reality. You can update the images whenever you have a new goal.

3. Set up reminders

Getting discouraged and caught up in negative emotions is easy on any journey. Being your own cheerleader is essential, but some days it's more difficult than others.

During coaching calls, more often than not, I find myself reminding you of how much you are worth and that you can do it. Some girls told me that, if they could, they would call me every day for the motivational dose I give them. So I thought of a way to be with you every day (me, or the person who inspires you the most, if you prefer to imagine that it is Miuccia Prada who tells you everything's ok!)

Set up reminders on your smartphone that recur every day at various times of the day (except on weekends when you need a well-deserved rest), and write quotes that motivate and remind you once again of your goal:

"I can do it," "I'm enough," "I'm a stylist and I work in New York," "I see you are a little down, but it's all in your head. Keep going." "Today will be great." "I'll do it anyway."

Imagine all of these pop-ups throughout your days that remind you where you want to go and make you smile (because let's be honest, if someone else saw our phones they would almost certainly think we're crazy, and even the humor of that will uplift your mood).

4. Shopping Rewards

Even though the focus of this book is your career, we're still talking about fashion, so I'm sure that at least once a month you add something new to your wardrobe, and at least once a week you visit your favorite online stores to check the new arrivals and add some items to your list. From today on, buy something after you've achieved a goal or taken action towards it. For example:

I'll only buy that new perfume when I have contacted all thirty fashion companies/people that I have on the list.

I will purchase this new coat only if, at the end of the month, I have applied for five internships or jobs every day.

I will write five articles and, as soon as I've sent all the emails and pitched the magazines, I'll buy myself my favorite cake!

This practice will not only keep you motivated, but it will make you feel satisfied because you will earn a reward that is well-deserved for the work you did.

When you get a job, your salary compensates you for the work done. But job hunting is a job itself! It's only fair that you deserve some credit for your commitment to get a job. So even if no one pays you for your job search, you can reward yourself by treating yourself with something new to pay yourself for your hard work.

• • • • • • • • • • • • • • • • • • •

The right mindset will push you to take action every day, not to give up, and keep moving forward until you have reached your goal. These four practices will help you enormously to maintain that dose of motivation and inspiration you need to remember where you are going. The first two chapters in this section have been very practical. You may want to read them again and come back in a few months, or whenever you feel you need to, to get back on track with your life. These practices will help you live your life to the fullest by becoming who you want to be and accomplishing your goals.

I would be so happy if you would like to share your career goals in fashion with me. Tag me at @glamobserver on Instagram or write me at giada@glamobserver.com and share your mood boards and shopping rewards with me :)

9

BE CONSISTENT

just like with your everyday face cream

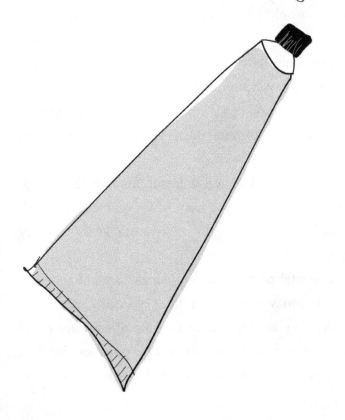

There is a fundamental concept behind the four practices I have just shown you. They are all based on one common thing: the fact that you repeat them on a daily basis. I started the previous chapter by telling you that the fundamental problem related to not being able to achieve a goal lies precisely in the fact that we leave it there on that note, agenda, or wherever we wrote it down, without doing anything. Taking action is essential, but even more important than taking action is being consistent.

Let me explain.

When you decide you want to get stronger, you go to the gym, but if you only go a couple of times you won't notice any difference. Just as eating salad one day won't make you healthier. Have you ever heard someone tell you to use a face cream once and you will see results?

The point is that you don't see results from the things you do just once or twice, but from the things you do every single day, consistently.

Your goals require multiple and different attempts in order to be achieved. Whatever goal you have set for yourself, you won't reach it by taking occasional action. You must take action every single day.

The most successful people and companies have not gotten to where they are today overnight. Often, especially with social media, we discover someone when they are already advanced in their career or the brand has already become popular. You admire those people and brands and tend to compare yourself to them, wanting to quickly achieve what they have built for years without you noticing. But behind every editor, stylist, CEO, designer, and successful brand, there are months and years of perseverance, dedication, and a lot of work. If they got where they are today it is because when they were where you are now, they made a choice to be consistent and not stop until they got what they wanted.

Each of us expects immediate results from our actions. We expect to be called back after just one job application, to lose weight after just one hour of jogging, to receive answers after just one email sent, and to have wonderful, luminous skin after applying one face mask.

But the real world doesn't work like that. And the real world includes your career as well.

If you apply for a few jobs one week and then take a break and start up again after a month, you probably won't see results. If you send a few emails to companies, stylists, photographers, and stop after the first four people haven't responded to you, you won't see results. If you pitch your articles to magazines and after the first five emails you get discouraged and stop pitching, you most likely will not get results.

Obviously, I am not saying that it is impossible to achieve something on the first attempt: the first company you applied for might hire you, the only person you email might get back to you, the first day you launch your new product it might just sell out. It happened to some students of Break into the Fashion

Industry. However, while having a positive attitude and being confident is important, we cannot leave anything to chance. We need to be more pragmatic and realistic.

We are not here to do things once and wait with our fingers crossed for the call from the two companies you have just applied for. If that happens, then awesome. But in the meantime, you are not waiting for that call, you are already customizing your CV to apply for other job offers and writing new cover letters to contact other companies. You are already writing a new article to submit to a magazine, and contacting other stylists to see if anyone will accept your request to become their assistant.

It's not easy, you have to be consistent, show up every morning, and take action every single day even when you don't see results yet.

But imagine what it would be like to go to work every morning, happy to do your job? What would it feel like to have made your dream come true? Being consistent is essential.

All the people I interviewed who work in fashion told me that they had to go through many NOs before getting a YES. Yes to a job application, yes to an article pitch, yes to an offer to become someone's assistant. Gisele Bündchen, yes, that Gisele, the supermodel, was rejected forty-two times before finally being cast in an Alexander McQueen fashion show in 1998 at the age of sixteen. Gisele received forty-two rejections. Forty-two!

If all the fashion industry professionals you see today weren't consistent and continued to pursue their dreams despite everything, they wouldn't have gotten the job they have today. If with Glam Observer I had stopped publishing articles every single day even when, for many months, there were just a dozen people reading them, I would not be here writing this book.

Being consistent is as fundamental as it is difficult. But I want you to finish this book with the tools you need for a career in fashion, and being consistent is one of them. So now I want to explain to you how you can become consistent.

Let's go back to the cream story we mentioned above.

At a certain point in our life, more or less around our teenage years, we added a new step to our morning routine. Aware of the fact that wearing a cream every morning is necessary to have beautiful skin, prevent aging, breakouts, etc ... we chose to wear it every single day. And so we made that action part of our routine. We do it religiously on a daily basis, rain or shine.

I've tested that the only way to make sure you do something on a daily basis and are therefore consistent is to turn that action into a habit.

Let's make a few examples to make everything more clear and simple:

GOAL	ACTION	HABIT
Grow your connections	Networking	Reach out to 3 fashion professionals <u>everyday</u>
Get a job in fashion	Apply for jobs	Apply for 5 jobs <u>everyday</u>
Work with a stylist	Email or send a DM	Email 4 stylists <u>everyday</u>
Write for a fashion magazine	Reach out to editors and publications	Pitch 6 articles to 6 publications <u>per week</u>

Someone once told me: "You suggested networking with those who work in fashion through Instagram. I tried, but I didn't see any changes." The first thing I ask here is: "How long have you been applying this strategy? How long have you been networking? How many people have you reached out to?"

On average the answer is networking for 2 days / reaching out to 2-4 people.Students who instead thank me for changing their lives have not only applied all of the correct strategies, but do it over a period of time on a consistent basis.

What really makes a difference in your life is not the action itself, but how consistent you are.

The right strategies + consistency = Success

Like when you started doing your makeup one day and now you do it every morning, now it's time for you to introduce habits into your daily routine that make you the successful fashion industry professional you are meant to be. We already saw this concept in the previous chapter. What allowed me to see results was moving from writing down my goals and forgetting about them, to triggering a series of automatic mechanisms that remind me every day where I'm going and why. Today I automatically wake up and write a list of my goals, it has become a habit! Incorporating new habits can be tough for the first few days. It could take a bit of extra effort in the beginning to get used to the change, but it's nothing someone powerful like you can't handle. Ready to welcome a new, more confident, and powerful you? Let's start with the first few hours of your days.

10

ANNA WINTOUR
WAKES UP
BETWEEN
4-5:30a.m.

HOW ABOUT

YOU?

There are so many books out there that talk about the endless benefits of a morning routine. *The Miracle Morning* is the one I read about five years ago when I first discovered and approached this practice. Apparently, it's something magical that actually works. All successful people religiously rely on their morning routine and consider it the most precious part of their day. So my curiosity and ambition to become successful led me to try it, and I must say that I noticed a huge difference.

The morning routine is especially popular with entrepreneurs, but I believe this practice can be beneficial for everyone, including those who work in fashion, from interns to CEOs. So, if you've already heard of a morning routine but have never considered it a reasonable option for you, now is the time to do it.

Anna Wintour, editor in chief of *Vogue* since 1988, artistic director for Condé Nast, and the most influential person in the fashion industry, wakes up between 4 and 5:30 a.m., reads both British and American news, plays tennis, and has breakfast at Starbucks before heading to the office at 8 a.m.

Diane von Furstenberg, another fashion industry icon, starts her day at 6 a.m. to meditate for about ten minutes and do yoga. She then has breakfast and starts checking her emails while also reading the newspapers: *New York Times*, *Financial Times*, *WWD*, *Business of Fashion*.

The reason why more and more people, including me, rely on a morning routine, is because the way you start your day affects the rest of it, as well as your mood.

Starting the day off right makes you feel happier and more motivated throughout the day.

Having a morning routine means that you wake up earlier than the usual time, not to get to the office before time but to have one or two more hours to do activities that make you feel better. The reason to fulfill these activities early in the morning and not leave them to accomplish later in the day is mainly because it is important to set the right mood to face a new day but also because it is probably the only time of day when you can focus on yourself without being interrupted or disturbed by other people, emails, social media, or any notifications.

The morning routine is a formula: which activities to include depends on your priorities. Heach of us has different needs, so to start the day off on the right foot and with ample motivation, we need to choose the activities that make us feel better; that's why each person's morning routine will naturally be different.

I admire Anna Wintour, but I don't think it would work for me to wake up at 4 a.m. I go to bed between 11-12 p.m., so four hours of sleep would be unsustainable in the long run.

After five years of experimenting, I've found my ideal formula.

I'll tell you how I set up my morning routine so you can use it as a reference.

I started by considering the activities successful people do when they wake up:

· Meditate
· Workout
· Read books
· Listen to podcasts
· Have breakfast
· Read the news
· Check emails
· Take a bath
· Write in a diary
· Practice gratitude
· Work on a personal project before going to work
· Attend online courses

I then started thinking about what things made me feel good, as well as my goals.

Being able to work out is important to me, not only because I have a very sedentary life and spend ten hours at a desk behind a computer, but above all because I know that physical activity has benefits not only for the body but also for the mind. I realize that with just thirty minutes of exercise, my whole day goes much better, I am happier and more productive. I don't train to lose weight, for me this concept doesn't work well early in the morning, but I see it more as a ritual to take care of myself, make my body stronger, and relieve stress. The formula that works for me is a daily thirty-minute workout, but everyone should choose the one that makes them feel best: a one-hour workout, only training three mornings, or twenty minutes a day. You can choose to go to the gym, take pilates or yoga classes online, swimming lessons, go for a run, or watch videos on YouTube, for example.

I want and need to learn new things to share tips on Glam Observer, improve my consultations, and learn about new marketing and business strategies.

There is never enough time. I would like to have many more hours available in the day especially for reading, listening to podcasts, attending courses, and watching webinars. Unfortunately, I never find the time to do these things because of all the work I have to do, so for me multitasking is essential. So in the morning, during those thirty minutes of training, I try to listen to a podcast about fashion, business, or career, or if I'm on my home exercise bike, I read in the meantime. There are those who cannot move without music, but I am a fan of multitasking, so I don't mind if I watch videos, read, or listen to a podcast while working out, cooking, going to the grocery store, taking a shower or driving. As I said, every routine is different. Maybe you need to listen to music while you go for a run and prefer to listen to a podcast during your lunch break because you like to take notes. To make it work you have to choose what is best for yourself.

Even when I'm not on the exercise bike, I try to read a career or business book for twenty minutes in the morning, and spend five minutes writing the list of my goals that we talked about in the first chapter. Then I typically read emails and check social media while having breakfast. Unfortunately, as soon as I open my eyes, I quickly check my emails to see if there is something urgent, but I would like to lose this bad habit of looking at my phone as soon as I wake up, and use it only to choose a podcast to listen to, postponing everything else until after my workout. I don't read the newspapers in the morning because I live in Italy, so the news from the US and London is not yet available when I wake up, and so I do this later in the day. But if I lived somewhere else, it would definitely be in my morning routine.

The most important thing when you want to practice this morning routine is to be consistent. I know that setting the alarm an hour or two earlier seems difficult and that rather than starting the day off well it might feel like you are starting it off badly because you wanted to sleep, but I assure you that the feeling of satisfaction at the end of it will pay off. You will be grateful for that hour dedicated to yourself and after a while you'll even look forward to your morning hours!

The fact that before you even get to the office, you have done so many things that make you happy and that you don't have to worry about during the day, will make you feel great. If for any reason I skip my morning routine, I feel guilty and become less productive that day because I spend it thinking about when I will be able to do those things that I missed. On those mornings when I don't want to get up (because it also happens to people who have practiced a morning routine for years) I just think about how I will feel when I finish my morning routine. And then I get up!

As we have already said, what will help you succeed in life and your career is your mindset. The morning routine will help you work on your mindset by giving it that dose of optimism, motivation, and knowledge you need to act toward the achievement of your goals and become the best version of yourself.

Wanting to improve yourself, learn new things, and stay up-to-date is necessary, and doing it daily will put you on the right path. Fashion is a fast-changing sector and being curious is key. Setting aside time every day for learning, listening to podcasts, reading books and magazines, and attending courses is an essential practice that should be done not only while looking for a job but also when you are working for a company.

Having a morning routine is perhaps even more essential when you have gotten a job and your free time will be much more limited. You will spend your whole day working, and in the evening you will be tired or there will be an unexpected project that keeps you at the office, or an event or dinner that you have to attend, and you skip your plans to go to the gym, take an online class, read, or cook. And as much as you love your job in the long run, you will miss taking time for yourself and you'll want to carve out hours in which you do what you like and do not just think about work 24/7. Your morning routine will also help you to keep stress under control both during the job search phase and once you start working.

Sometimes things can be stressful in fashion. Some people take fashion so seriously that it's as if they consider their work to be as important as doctors who are saving lives. Obviously, that's not the case, but those who think this way tend to put a lot of pressure on themselves and others. Unfortunately, there are many sad stories from fashion professionals and designers with mental health issues. Burnout is a real thing in fashion.

The definition of burnout, according to HelpGuide, is a state of emotional, physical, and mental exhaustion caused by excessive and prolonged stress. It occurs when you feel overwhelmed, emotionally drained, and unable to meet constant demands.

Obviously not every day is so stressful in fashion and above all it depends so much on the company and your team, but during peak periods like fashion week things could get more hectic and your morning hour will make you face everything with more grit, optimism, and motivation.

When you have a morning routine you feel like you are in control of your life. By doing different things and moving from one activity to another, your unconscious will reassure you as you cross all those things off your list—working out, reading a book, listening to a podcast, taking a language course, starting your side-hustle, writing your blog, filming videos for your YouTube channel, working on your brand/business—that you can do it all and tackle everything planned for that day. Your mind is programmed to keep completing one task after another throughout the day. Your office to-do list will no longer seem so long, and you will have a positive approach to finding a solution and getting to the end of each task as smoothly as you did with your morning routine.

Don't you occasionally see someone on Instagram stories, who seems like they can do 1,000 things while you find it challenging to do one? They don't have any special powers, they just have the motivation and find a way to do everything and you have it too! Wouldn't you be happier if you lived your life to the fullest doing ALL the things you want instead of deciding to do just one thing because you don't have time?

One hour in the morning is enough to totally change your life.
- 5 minutes to get out of your pajamas and put on your yoga pants
- 30 minutes of training (yoga, pilates, going for a run)
- 20 minutes of reading
- 5 minutes to write your goals list

You will see that you will become much more positive, happy, satisfied, motivated, optimistic, confident, informed, and less stressed, and you will feel that you are living your life to the fullest.

Try to anticipate your alarm going off tomorrow. The first week will be hard, but trust me, try to focus on how you feel at the end of your routine and it will motivate you to get up, even when you don't feel like it.

At the time of writing this book, the hashtag #*mydreammorningroutine* is still free, so let's use it to share our morning routines ☺ Tag me at @glamobserver .

11

THE MARVELOUS SEVEN

In this part of the book, we are focusing on the habits to incorporate into your routines that will contribute to your career. Although what characterizes the routine is repetition, this does not mean that the activities that are part of it must always be the same over time. It is indeed important to introduce new habits when necessary and adapt them to your goals. Maybe the morning routine we just talked about is completely new to you and will be part of your new habits from today. The habits I am going to tell you about may be totally new to you, or you might have heard of them, or already experienced some of them. Some may seem uncomfortable or you might think they're not for you, but the goal of these habits is to get you out of your comfort zone.

As president Thomas Jefferson said:

"If you want something you've never had, you must be willing to do something you've never done."

Most of us are afraid to try something new, perhaps because we are afraid of failing, because we don't like to feel uncomfortable, we don't like change, or simply because we are used to doing something a certain way and we don't want to change our own established habits.

But the truth is that if you want to see a change in your life, if you want to grow, if you want to achieve something you don't currently have, you have to get out of your comfort zone by adding different habits to your usual practices.

To explain myself better, let's say that you have been applying for jobs or internships in fashion for a while without results: companies do not respond to you and you are still wondering what is wrong with your applications, or worse, what is wrong with you. Well, obviously there is nothing wrong with you. It's just that if you want a different result, or want to get something that you don't have, you should do things differently.

Whenever I'm scared to do something new, I remember this quote from from author, motivational speaker and entrepreneur, Jack Canfield:

"Everything you want is on the other side of fear."

and I decide to do it anyway. We often use fear to justify ourselves: "I didn't do it because I was afraid."

For the last couple of years, however, I've learned to accept the fear because I know that it is a natural human emotion and, although we cannot choose whether or not to be afraid, we can choose to carry on despite the fear.

I've realized that if I wait for the fear to go away, the opportunity will go away too and if I don't take action, I will never get what I want. I also know that the best things in life aren't easy, so it's normal for me to feel a sense of risk when I want to try something new.

And you know what? Most of the best things I've achieved so far are those I've done by pushing myself and doing something that scared me, getting out of my comfort zone.

These are all habits that I have developed over time and that have helped me enormously in my career. I specifically used the word "habit" and not "strategy" for these Marvelous Seven, because they must become part of your daily life and not just something you use when you need it.

IF YOU DON'T AKS, YOU DON'T GET

In the office when I was still an intern, I started getting more assignments and responsibilities as soon as I started asking for them. I did not wait for my boss to entrust me with new tasks; as soon as I understood my job, the jobs of the whole team, and my boss's, I asked if I could take care of something new and relieve some of the burden from my boss's job. Today, asking is still a habit even with Glam Observer. I send emails on top of emails on top of emails for anything that I want.

If you don't ask, you won't get. It's very simple. You see someone doing your dream job, traveling, going to photo shoots, writing for the best fashion magazines, and you think how lucky they are that they were offered that job. In 90% of cases, when you see a person working on something fashion-related (assisting a stylist, working backstage at a fashion show), it is because they asked for it. Unless you are Suzy Menkes or Elizabeth Stewart, no one will come to offer you a job simply because you are at the beginning of your career. You have to get out there, show your work, and introduce yourself to the world.

Whatever you want, despite any doubts, don't be afraid to ask for it. There are no silly requests or questions, the only thing you need to worry about is asking at the right time, not when people are busy and might miss your request (like during fashion week for example, or the minute before your boss walks into a meeting), and always be polite when asking.

Do you want to work with a stylist?

Have you written an article and would like to publish it in a magazine?

Are you looking for an internship?

Do you want to take on more responsibility at work?

Do you want to work remotely?

Do you want to manage the social media of your favorite brand on Instagram?

Do you want to meet someone for a coffee?

Would you like to take care of a new project?

Do you want someone to look at your portfolio?

Your favorite photographer already has an assistant and you would like to ask if you can become the second assistant?

You've just seen a new brand or project that you like and want to be a part of it?

Do you want to help backstage at a fashion show?

Ask.

I know it's not easy, especially for someone who is an introvert like me. I have always been afraid to ask for anything. I always thought that if anyone needed me, they knew what my skills were and where to find me, so they would send me an email or call.

But that's not really how it works. How do people know who you are and what you are capable of if you don't go out there and explain your skills? How do others know that you are interested in a new project or job? Don't assume that people know what you want or think.Nobody will knock on your door with an internship, a job, a collaboration, or a project served on a silver platter.

It is your responsibility to make things happen.
And you are also responsible for anything
that doesn't happen.

Don't wait for a job to magically appear or for someone to offer you something. If you know what you want, you have to go out there and get it. The only person who will hinder you *is YOU,* which means that you are also the *only one* who will be able to access things.

Send emails like it's your job, because in the end, it will get you one!

Ask those you know, the network you will build after you have read the networking chapter, as well as strangers, your boss, coworkers, friends, former classmates or former colleagues, people you will meet at events.

And ask yourself every day if what you are doing today is getting you closer to where you want to be tomorrow.

EVERY NO IS JUST A NOT YET

"A million girls would kill for that job" I guess you remember this quote from *The Devil Wears Prada.* There are so many people out there who want a position in fashion that, as you can imagine, it is very unlikely that you will receive a YES to all your requests, emails, and applications. The positive side is that it means there is something for everyone! If someone says no to you, they said yes to someone else and, even though our minds might not accept it, like it happened to them, it's going to happen to you!

Asking and putting yourself out there as suggested in Habit #1 also implies receiving several "nos," but this is the beauty of this process, and it is here we see who survives and who gives up. It is true you will receive many "nos," but you need only one YES to change your life! Rather than focusing on the nos you might receive when you apply, or when you contact a stylist, editor, or company, when you ask for something think that sooner or later there will be a YES. Focus on your YES that is to come and let it be your fuel that pushes you forward. You don't want to be the one who quits.

You choose. You can choose to be blocked and discouraged by one, two, or ten nos, or choose to go on despite everything to get to where you want to be.

Every time I achieve something, I look back and thank the person I was a few weeks, months, or years ago who didn't get discouraged by nos and today has finally received a YES. All the people you see in fashion today who you admire have received many nos, but the secret of their success has been simply just not giving up.
Each no is just a NOT YET.

If you reach out to someone or apply for a job and get turned down or get no response, it doesn't mean you'll never work for your dream company or shouldn't contact anyone else. You can apply again for the next job opportunity (even in the same company where they've just rejected you), you can write to the next person, or you can analyze what you did wrong, fix it, and try again.

> Your strategies may fail,
> but you are not a failure.

This book is not just a career manual; I also want to tell you objectively how the dynamics in this industry work so that you are prepared and know how to react. I am telling you right now that you will receive nos, because everyone receives them, so don't let it bother you and above all do not let it stop you, just be ready to receive them and move on.

THE ART OF FOLLOWING UP

One day a well-known person in fashion told me that she only considers candidates who follow up because it is a way to test if the person is really interested in that job or they are just randomly applying for different jobs. In this way, she automatically makes a first selection. Personally, it is something that I also do with Glam Observer; I wait for that second email. Conversely, I do the same thing in my own work; I have a day of the week dedicated to following up! It works like this for everyone.

Fashion people are always busy and get hundreds of emails every day, so although we are always connected and check our smartphones every second, your email or application could arrive at a time when it is read on-the-go or end up at the bottom of the list quickly.

Whether you have sent an internship request, you are waiting for a feedback after a job interview, or you have contacted someone for an informational interview, don't forget to follow up. Make it a habit, from today on every email you send will be followed by another email if you do not hear back.

KEEP LEARNING

"This job requires knowledge of French / Photoshop / Excel / InDesign / Wordpress / SEO / ... I can't apply because I don't know it."

This is the most detrimental attitude you could have when you are job seeking. No one already has the entire list of requirements listed by the company at the time of application, but if there is one thing that is true it is that YOU can learn everything. If after I publish this book, I still receive emails saying you can't apply because you lack something, I swear I will scream at you. Do you really want to give up and not apply for a job that seems made just for you, just because in that moment you are missing something you can learn? If you have this book in your hands, I'm sure not.

YOU ARE YOUR MOST POWERFUL CAREER TOOL TO GET THAT JOB IN FASHION.

EVERYTHING STARTS WITH YOU. HOW AND WHO YOU WILL BE AND WHAT YOU WILL KNOW TOMORROW

Your mindset from today should be like this:

"Not yet, but I'll figure it out. I can learn it."

"Okay, I've never heard of it, but I'm sure I'll be able to find out more soon."

"Can you use this Excel function?" "Yes! I'll look for it immediately on Google."

"You need to speak French to work here." "I will download an app and take an online course to learn it very quickly."

You should make learning a daily habit, so don't do it just when you need it right before applying for a job or when your boss assigns you a new task.

It is no coincidence that for the morning routine I suggest (and I also do this too) activities that include ongoing learning such as listening to podcasts, reading for twenty minutes, and taking online courses. It takes very little time every single day. You'd be surprised at how many things you can learn from a single podcast.

It doesn't matter if you are a student, intern, assistant, junior, senior, or CEO; if you want to keep growing and succeeding, you will always have to learn something new and gain new skills, even when you are not asked.

There is no need to return to university or get an MBA.

All the practical things I need for work, and the best information I've learned relating to fashion, career, and business, I have learned by myself, on Google, on YouTube, through books and podcasts. I would never give up my daily dose of podcasts, books, or courses because I know that without them the whole engine stops.

Whenever I feel unmotivated, uninspired, don't know what to write about, or feel stuck in any way, I no longer try to force myself to get inspired because I know that I will continue staring at the screen and the hours will pass without results. I hate wasting time, so rather than forcing myself to produce something at any cost, I just read for a while, listen to a podcast, or watch a video on YouTube and immediately I get my inspiration and motivation back.

The more you know, the more ideas you will get. Even if at that moment you think that information may not be very useful to you, you have assimilated that knowledge and, at the right time, you can count on it: you could be assigned a new project at work because you had a great idea or because you can say you took a course on that subject a few months ago.

You should be obsessed with your job or future job and want to know more and more.

Learn everything about your job and even beyond. Miuccia Prada, in an interview at the end of the first fashion show co-created with Raf Simons, presented in September 2020 during the digital Milan fashion week, said that you have to "study, study, study" to work in fashion ... "reading literature, looking at art, watching movies." You don't have to learn only about fashion or styling; learn about anything that is relevant or interesting to you: journalism, design, buying … you should have transversal skills.

Fashion companies appreciate people who have more skills, are curious, and always want to learn. Interns very often deal with different activities at the same time and it is therefore necessary to have more skills and keep studying in order to ask for more responsibilities.

Obviously, increasing one's knowledge raises self-confidence proportionally. Most of the times when you have doubts it's because you don't believe you have the right skills to do something, whether it's applying for a job because you're missing some requirements, accepting a project because it's new, or having to work with a new tool. I have written an entire chapter on how to become more confident that we'll see later, but meanwhile, if you needed one more reason to introduce a daily dose of learning into your habits, now you have it.

The more you know, the more multitalented you become, and it's a skill that is increasingly fundamental in fashion. Following the pandemic that hit the world in 2020, this concept has become even more fundamental.

We are still in the pandemic when I write this. The whole world has changed. No one was prepared for the day our leaders would stop life as we knew it to let us know that the entire nation would be closed overnight. Stores, companies, factories … everything had to shut down and close.

This was a huge blow not only to the fashion industry but most industries around the world. Fashion weeks were canceled;

production stopped; designers had to choose fabrics from a webcam; many people lost their jobs; all meetings, buying, and events were held online; showrooms were organized digitally; fashion school graduates presented their collections online and some graduated without showing a collection and with no chance to celebrate; many internships were postponed or canceled; and companies froze the hiring process.

With the entire fashion industry and the world paralyzed and forced to close, those (both companies and individuals) who were able to continue working and survive this unprecedented event were those who were able to reinvent themselves and adapt to new ways of working from home and online. Zara, the fast fashion giant, sent its products to the models to shoot from home, where they also had to improvise as their own makeup artists, photographers, and hair stylists to shoot the editorials for the e-commerce team, who had to upload on the website to continue selling collections online. Fashion photographers organized photo shoots at home by shooting still lifes, stylists have done consultations via video calls, and on and on.

Increasing your skill set and continuing to learn new things is no longer an option, but an essential trait for your career.

With all the online courses, podcasts, books, and endless knowledge you can find through Google, we have everything we need at our fingertips. You have no excuse not to learn something new every single day.

Constant learning stimulates the mind and makes you smart and adaptable. Make it a habit.

SURROUND YOURSELF WITH OTHER FASHION PROFESSIONALS

The famous businessman Jim Rohn said, "You are the average of the five people you spend most of your time with." The people we surround ourselves with are the biggest influence on our behavior, attitudes, and outcomes. If the people you spend most of your time with do nothing but complain, you probably will too. If they are negative people, you will probably develop that mindset. If they are people who eat healthy and exercise regularly, most likely you will too.

Surround yourself with positive people, people who have self-confidence, people who don't get scared when faced with the first difficulty, resolute people who always find a solution, people who help you learn from your mistakes rather than blame them, and people who always see the glass half full, inspiring you to do the same.

But before you even surround yourself with people who inspire and motivate you, step away from the people who don't support your ambitions and stop following all those people who make you feel bad about yourself (although in the previous chapter we saw how you shouldn't compare yourself to those who are already successful, but instead analyze their path to realize that they too started where you are now), or you will be influenced by two opposite mindsets that will not give you the right balance. If, when you check Instagram, some people make you feel bad about yourself and you close the app feeling worse than you were before, you should reconsider the people you follow. Your social feed should be a breath of motivation and inspiration, not a place where you feel like you are not lucky enough or don't deserve the same happiness or experiences.

Since you want to work in fashion, surround yourself and follow people who work in this industry, reach out to other interns, and spend time with people who inspire you, people who motivate you to give your best. If you've ever attended one of my fashion panels you should have felt that vibrating energy in the room. When you bring together people who share the same passion, enthusiasm, and goals, magic happens. Attend events and you'll read later in the Networking chapter about how to get in touch with fashion industry professionals.

It generally happens that when you join a company, especially as an intern, your boss or someone else on the team becomes your mentor. Not just someone who explains how to do your job but someone who guides you on your career path in fashion. Finding a mentor is a gold. People will take you under their wing to help you grow, recommend you for your next job, explain how the dynamics work, and guide you in making the best choices.

Not everyone has this luck. My mentors are not mentors who have followed me personally; they have no idea who I am. I never even sent them an email because they are very important people like Sara Blakely from Spanx (Hi Sara, if you ever read this book, write me!).

They are kind of like idols whose books I read, and whose every interview I listen to get to know them (even without knowing them in person), and learn from them even if they were not actually mentoring me. I love that just by following someone online today, you can feel like you know them.

I am honored to be a mentor to so many special people in the Glam Observer community. So if you are lucky to find such a person at work, get as much out of it as possible, or if you don't, just continue to be guided by the advice and stories of people that you read in books, listen to in podcasts, or see online.

A recap:

1. Unfollow people (in real life and online) who make you feel bad and who do not want to build you up but do the opposite

2. Surround yourself with people who inspire you, who encourage you to bring out the best in yourself, and people who work in fashion

3. Find mentors in your office, at school, online, and in the community

DON'T LIVE IN FEAR,
BELIEVE IN ABUNDANCE

We have almost reached the end of this second part of the book and are about to begin the third. In the following part we will talk about your fashion career tools including your CV, the job interview, and your network. If it is true that these tools are necessary to get you a job it is also true that having a perfect CV and meeting people is not enough if you continue to have the wrong mindset that will unconsciously block you.

How many times have you looked at others, thinking they are so lucky and that you will never reach their level of success or similar opportunities because there is no room for everyone in fashion? This means you are living with a scarcity mindset where you believe there is not enough for everyone, that life is unfair, and that nothing can really change, or that with you these things don't work. With this mindset you reinforce the negative signals in your brain by continuing to respond to life as if the worst is about to happen.

Just to give you a practical example: When you get the email from the recruiter letting you know they're moving on to other candidates, your scarcity mindset says, "I didn't get this job because I'm not good enough. I'll never get a job!" or "I should just get this job/give up on working in fashion and do something else."

Shift your mindset from scarcity to abundance. People with an abundance mindset focus on the endless opportunities available in life. They choose to focus on the positive rather than the negative, and they believe there is an abundance of everything in life, be it more time, more money, better relationships, more resources, and more opportunities.

An abundance mindset says:
"My dream job is still out there waiting for me. I will keep searching, I will keep applying. I can do better."

A stuck mentality thinks: "How many applications am I sending?!?!" while what you should focus on is:

"How good are the applications that I send?"

Shift your mindset towards positive thinking and abundance.

STOP STOPPING

I remember when I was little, one of my favorite cartoons was *Kim Possible*, a high school student/agent who every day had an enemy to face in order to save the world. I don't remember the exact words, but she used to say something like "Impossible is not my last name," meaning that she could do anything. I don't know if I already had it inside of me, but I still remember that quote. I must have been about ten years old, but at that moment it became the motto of my life.

I've always preferred heroines to princesses for their ability to find a solution in every situation. I'm also a fan of Lara Croft in fact. I joke about it when someone, even from my family, asks me "What's the problem?" and I answer, "I don't have problems, only solutions," but in the end I think I really believe it. Of course I know there are problems. Each of us has them. I had them when I was looking for a job and I have them every single day now as an entrepreneur. I don't always have this positive attitude, I happen to have some good cries sometimes, but I think that deep down, in the end, I firmly believe that there really is a solution to everything and it is this belief that got me where I am today and it will keep me going in the future. I know that crying won't solve anything. I have to get up, roll up my sleeves, and take care of the problem even if at that moment it seems very difficult, I have no idea where to start and I just want to have a magic wand to get to the solution already. I'm sure you've complained about something that in the end you had to do anyway, and you came to a solution. How you managed to do that thing you can apply to everything else. Google is my best friend for everything. Many times, even when I was working as an intern, I said yes and figured out a way to do it.

I've always tried to find a solution as if there was no plan B. Some people say you always have to have a plan B, it's safer.

I see it differently.

Having a plan B means having doubts about plan A and if you don't really believe in something then you increase the chances of failing.

Many have asked me what my plan B was if Glam Observer didn't go well. I always replied that I didn't have a plan B, that I would make it work. And every day I still wake up and work hard to make my plan A work. I know that it is not always easy, that you have to be brave and decide to do it even though it can be scary, but this habit of believing that there is a solution to everything and that nothing is impossible—from finding your first job to dealing with the work your boss has just assigned you—will keep you going.

To quote Nike "Just do it."

Planning is super interesting and exciting. Maybe now you have your goal and a list of five actions in order to achieve it, and you think that the habits we talked about are all very useful.
But the step between thinking and doing is enormous.
Too many times we know what the necessary steps are but then we tend to procrastinate.

I didn't write this book to tell you some things that you may want to try someday. I wrote this book with the aim of giving you results, and the only way to get them is to act, but not one day, not in a week, not tomorrow. Do It Now.

Don't be a dreamer anymore, be a doer today and stop stopping.

PART III

Fashion Career Tools

12

HOW TO GET A JOB IN FASHION,

Tom Ford enrolled at New York University in 1979 to study art history. After a year, he dropped out of school and moved to Los Angeles to pursue an acting career. A few years later, he returned to New York and enrolled at the Parsons School of Design to study architecture. During his last year there he realized he wanted to work in fashion. In 1985, after graduating from Parsons with a degree in architecture, Ford wanted to enter the world of fashion by working with the designer Cathy Hardwick, not only because she was a famous fashion designer, but to learn the business side of a fashion company as well.

Ford called Hardwick's office every day for a month straight.

Hoping to finally get rid of this person who called every day, Hardwick herself answered the phone and asked Ford what was the earliest available time he could meet for a job interview. A little less than two minutes later, Ford showed up in her office. He had called from the lobby.

Hardwick recalls their memorable first meeting:

"I had every intention of not giving him hope. I asked him who his favorite European designers were. He replied: "Armani and Chanel."

"Why Armani?" I asked. "Because you were wearing something Armani." Tom said."

Lazaro Hernandez, one of the designers behind the brand Proenza Schouler together with Jack McCollough, shared an extraordinary anecdote about Anna Wintour at a conference at the Institute of Contemporary Art in Boston some years ago. Hernandez was still a student when one day he found himself on the same flight as Anna Wintour heading from Miami to New York. He was sitting in economy class with his mother, and during the flight he decided to write a note on a napkin for Anna Wintour, in which he expressed his passion for fashion and his favorite designer Michael Kors. He decided to go to first class and give his message to Anna Wintour. She was resting, or maybe not (who can tell behind her dark glasses), so he decided to leave the napkin next to her, so they had no contact.

Two weeks later, Lazaro got a call from Michael Kors, telling him that Anna Wintour had given him a letter from a guy on the plane and that Kors should hire him as an intern. The rest is history.

I could have started this chapter explaining how to write your resume to get a job in fashion. But the reality is that these two stories represent the *real* way to get a job in fashion, and that I have been sharing for six years now: going beyond the standard application and exceed expectations.

Especially today that social media exposure has made the industry more transparent and popular than it was already, becoming more and more competitive.

Write your CV. Go online to check websites that post job vacancies. Look for the right job. Apply. Get an interview. Go the interview. Repeat. Get the job.

We wish it were as easy as that.

The standard job application process no longer works as well as it once did, in a competitive industry such as fashion. But you probably already know that getting a job in fashion is not that easy.

From LinkedIn you can see the number of people applying for a job offer. On average, for one of the most sought-after brands in the industry, around 200-300 people apply for the same job. If we then add those who apply on the official website of the brand and other job sites where the position is also posted, we arrive at a total of about 500 candidates on average for the same fashion job or internship.

As you can understand, getting noticed among 500 applicants is certainly not an easy thing and even a single mistake can put you out of the running since the company will have 499 other people to choose from.

Richard N. Bolles, in *What Color Is Your Parachute? 2020* writes:

"In today's world, whoever gets hired isn't necessarily the one who can do that job best; but, the one who knows most about how to get hired."

And it is absolutely true. I want you to understand this.

Do you remember when I told you that after the Break into the Fashion Industry course, students immediately start receiving responses from companies, are invited to interviews, and get jobs even though they are basically the same person as before and haven't acquired any new technical skills or work experience? Companies today aren't just looking for people who have studied at the best universities, but for someone who manages to demonstrate that they have that extra something that impresses them to the point of inviting you for a job interview.

Tom Ford didn't wait for Cathy Hardwick to open a position in order to apply and get a job there. He called the office every day.

Lazaro Hernandez was brave enough to go to Anna Wintour and leave a napkin, despite the fact that she ignored him.

Over the past years I have shared unconventional strategies with a similar approach to these two stories to get a job in fashion, because going beyond the standard application it is the only way to get noticed in a world full of talent and qualified people. It doesn't matter what you have studied or your previous experience.

While you will have to continue applying online and sending your CV, this is just one part of the process. If you have already tried to apply for a job or internship in fashion and have not seen results, it's probably time to change your strategies and introduce something that goes beyond the traditional schemes. Fashion is every day more and more competitive, let's add the fact that digital has changed the way companies evaluate and hire candidates, and let's also add global situations such as the 2020 pandemic in which jobs have decreased and competition has increased, and you will realize that the standard application alone does not hold up.

It doesn't hold up if you don't want to get stressed out and want to get into the fashion industry quickly. If you are willing to wait months, using the standard application may work sooner or later. But wasting so much time is not our goal.

Every time you apply for a job or internship from today on, always think: How can I amaze the company and show them that I'm the perfect person for the job?

Think BIG.

It is true that you do not have control over what a recruiter or company thinks about you, but you do have control over the actions you can take:

• Email a recruiter or manager
• Improve your CV and customize it exactly to the job offer, with a template that stands out so that the recruiter immediately says "Someone give me their number."
• Rewrite your cover letter
• Apply for multiple positions
• Explain to the company more clearly why they should hire you
• Be consistent
• Submit a portfolio or document that proves you are the perfect person for the job
• Invite those who work in fashion for a coffee, learn their story and their advice and get invited later for a job interview

In this part of the book I will show you the fashion career tools you'll need to get a job in fashion (I use the word "job" for convenience but all of the strategies mentioned also apply to internships).

We will start with fashion internships as they represent your entry into fashion regardless of what you have studied, and if you are lacking work experience. Then I will introduce a series of *new* tools useful for your career: wanting to work in fashion today and not considering using LinkedIn and Instagram (that have become the new resume), not leveraging your connections (you will learn how to build them from scratch), and not using a direct approach via email directly to a stylist, recruiter, editor, buyer ... means losing many opportunities.

But that's what I'm here for. After today you will not miss any opportunities, and even better, we will create them even where you think there are none.

13

YOUR ENTRY-TICKET
TO THE
FASHION INDUSTRY

If you ask me what's the # 1 tip I have for getting into the fashion industry, I would without a doubt say: do as many internships as you possibly can.

Internships represent your entry-ticket into the working world of fashion.

If you want to start a career in fashion, you will have to go through one or more internships. It doesn't matter which university or fashion school you have attended.

Even those who hold the most recognized positions in fashion today started with an internship.

It is common to hear stories of people who have obtained an internship because their mother's friend worked at a magazine, or the friend of her mother's friend had a fashion brand. When I started, I didn't have these kinds of connections. So all the strategies within this book, and that I have taught over the past years with Glam Observer, work also for people like me, who did not have even the slightest and distant link to someone who worked in fashion.

If you know someone who knows someone who works in fashion, then you might first start by spreading the word that you are looking for an internship.

Otherwise, or to simply be open to more opportunities, just follow the strategies I'm about to tell you.

To these questions:

How can I work in fashion without a fashion degree?

How do I get my first job in fashion?

How do I work in fashion if I have no experience?

Can I work in fashion without a degree?

How do I work in fashion when I am still a student?

How can I enter the industry as a new graduate?

I just graduated, should I pursue a master's degree or look for an internship?

There is always only one answer: look for a fashion internship.

What is an internship and what does an intern do?

An internship is a temporary work opportunity that companies or individuals offer to those who are students, newly graduated, or anyone with little or no experience or knowledge of the industry. Internships are an opportunity to learn what you will really need to do on the job. If you have considered what you've learned at university to be impractical and not relevant to the real world, internships will teach you what actually goes on at a fashion company.

Every career in fashion has an opportunity to intern, from buying to merchandising to designing to marketing ... so whatever your dream job is, there is an internship from which you can start.

Fashion interns do different things according to the department, the role, the company, and the people they are working for, but in general the main job of an intern is to support someone else's job (the boss) by taking care of basic activities.

All companies offer internships: from the most prestigious ones such as Dior, Chanel, Valentino, and Gucci, to online stores, showrooms, and startups. The good news is that internship opportunities are more available than full-time positions. Mainly because it is more advantageous for companies to hire an intern because there are many cost benefits compared to a full-time position.

In addition to companies, you can also do internships with people and become someone's assistant. This usually happens when you work with freelance professionals such as stylists, photographers, or graphic designers.

Who can do an internship?

Internships are divided into two main categories: internships for students to earn college credits, and internships that we'll define as "general" in which the company does not require the intern to be a student. You can apply for these internships if you didn't go to university, you're transitioning from one internship to another, or you've graduated recently. It's necessary therefore to read the job description for each internship carefully to see if they are reserved for students before applying.

So, to recap, internships are for:

students

graduates

anyone with little or no work experience

Why do you need to intern?

1. To enter the working world of fashion

The main reason why you need internships is because they represent your ticket to the fashion industry. If you still have no experience, have just graduated, or are still studying (anything related to fashion or a traditional degree) there is no other way to get into this industry except to first intern.

2. To understand which fashion career is ideal for you

Internships, in addition to representing your entry into the fashion industry, are essential to understand what you really want to do. It often happens that you'll have an idea of a dream career and change it as soon as you enter the company. Only when you get inside the industry and start gaining experience, understanding how a company works, how it's organized and who does what, you can find the career that's really made for you. It is absolutely normal if you are doing an internship and you find that that job is not for you and you decide to change everything!

If you are undecided between two careers, doing two different internships will help you understand your preferences.

You may want to work as a stylist but you are undecided whether to become a celebrity stylist or work for a magazine or in e-commerce. Or you want to work in PR but you don't know yet if you prefer to work at a PR agency that manages various brands or to join the PR department of a company and work for a single brand. Trying out all the possible options through internships is the best way to understand what you want to do in practice.

But be careful before assuming that a job is not made for you. It often happens that some interns are asked to make photocopies or bring coffee; obviously these are not the main activities of the job. So if during your PR internship they ask you to do these things, it does not mean that working in communication is not for you. Rather, once you are in the office during the internship, observe your boss's work and the one of the people in your team to see if that's what you'd like to do, because in the future, you might be filling one of that roles. Look at what other departments and people are doing as well to find out if you might prefer another career, and to understand the business operation as a whole.

3. To build your first real fashion connections

Another key benefit of interning is that you will build your first in-person connections in the fashion industry. As we will see in the chapter dedicated to networking, relationships are so essential for your career. With an internship you are entering a company, you will meet your boss, your team, people from other departments, and people from other companies with whom you will have working relationships. One of your goals during the internship is to get to know and talk to as many people as possible. Arrive early in the morning for coffee and a chat with someone from another team; if you have some free time during your internship and your boss has no other work for you, ask someone else if you can help them so you build a connection and learn something new at the same time.

Establishing great relationships with your coworkers is critical not only to work well when you are there. You need to make as many connections as you can and keep in touch with everyone, even when your internship is over, for your next career opportunities. Your fellow intern or colleague might work somewhere else in three years and you might need their help.

Interning is therefore a spontaneous and simple way to networking.

4. To make it easier to get a full-time job

If a company has to choose between those who have just graduated from a prestigious university and those who already have a couple of internships under their belt, in 90% of the cases, they will choose the latter. So the more internships you do, the more opportunities you have to find a job. The ultimate goal of your internship should be to turn it into a full-time job.

It is much easier to join a company as an intern and turn that internship into a full-time job, rather than looking for a new job at a different company. Therefore, from the first day you enter as an intern, you must do everything possible so that the company is happy with your work and wants to keep you because you have become indispensable. Even if you don't like the company or your job, it does not mean that you have to do your job badly so that you don't get an offer. In fact, the goal is never to get fired.

Everyone in fashion knows everyone else. From the moment you step into the first fashion company, even as an intern, you have started building your reputation throughout the entire fashion industry. So don't assume that just because you're still an intern, no one will notice you. Do your job well even when you don't like it so much. In fashion, word travels fast, leave a good impression with everyone, not just with your boss but also with other interns or even the doorman.

Work hard and be ready to do whatever they ask you, even if it means making coffee. The better you do your job, even tasks that seem boring or too easy to you, the more responsibilities you will be assigned. Also remember that being kind is essential and will take you far in your career.

We'll talk more later on how to get noticed in a fashion office and how I turned an internship into something more.

When to do a fashion internship?

If you can do one or more internships while still in school it's ideal because is a great way to make your CV more appealing once you graduate and also to get a full-time job earlier.

So if you're reading this book while still in college, be sure to take advantage of internships while you're there.

It is common (unfortunately) that internships are often unpaid or pay very little. If you want to get a well-paying job after graduating, you should intern during your studies. I know it's not the easiest thing in the world to juggle your studies with a job, but many do this and if other people have done it, you can too. Furthermore when you consider that internships are key to getting a full-time job and on average a company requires a minimum of a 6 month to 1 year internship experience before offering a full-time job to someone, it's often worth it. Luckily this requirement doesn't necessarily have to be filled at the same company. Even if you can do four internships of three months each at different companies, you would still reach the total internship experience that you need to get a full-time job.

Some college degrees include an internship already in the curriculum, usually in the final year. But if that isn't required in your program, look for this opportunity yourself in your first, second, or third year of college.

A full-time internship is more difficult to manage while studying, but you may want to consider part-time internships instead. Part-time internships generally require the intern to work for about 2-3 days a week or just a half-day, so they are much easier to combine with your studies than a full-time internship. It is certainly not easy and requires sacrifices: studying during the weekend and in the evenings to make up for the days in which you work, but you know that the best things in life require a lot of hard work. Think about how satisfied you will feel when, the day after your graduation, a company is impressed by your CV because you managed to gain all this experience and above all to manage it while studying. Think of your classmates who partied every weekend, and will be starting an internship while you are already applying to full-time jobs. Also, when you are still in school your mind is in "student mode," so you're more open to taking on an unpaid internship during that time than you would be after graduating. By not excluding unpaid internships, you increase your chances of finding an internship because there are more options to choose from. When you graduate, everything becomes more difficult because you start applying filters during your job search: you are looking for an internship that pays at least enough to cover your expenses, and, since you have a degree now, you are looking for one that matches your title and therefore does not involve bringing coffee or making photocopies. It is absolutely understandable after years of studying to want a job that respects your degree. However, going through internships is the way to enter this industry and in fashion the stories of interns who fetch coffee and run personal errands for their boss (remember when Andy in *The Devil wears Prada* did the homework of Miranda's kids?) are not so rare. So if you haven't brought coffee or made photocopies during college, chances are you will when you graduate.

Even if you could afford to do unpaid internships after graduation, think about how much time you will save if you already had nine months or one year of an internship under your belt. You save a full year of internship experience that you would have to do as soon as you graduate. You're already ahead of the game which means you will be able to access prestigious and senior positions from a young age.

I would like to point out that I'm not on the side of companies that do not pay their interns, especially when it comes to big names in the industry who can afford it. So I'm not saying all these things to justify unpaid internships. I don't neither approve those who "exploit" their interns. I'm just objectively explaining the reality of entering the fashion industry and in some cases it also involves bringing coffee and doing an unpaid internship.

My goal is to prepare you to enter the fashion world and get you there well-equipped. The more you know, the more you understand how you have to handle some situations. If someone asks you to make photocopies during an internship, it's not that they think you can't do anything else, but because that's what they're used to.

A lot of how your internship is going to be, depends on the company, the job, and your boss. I had a positive internship experience. I had many responsibilities like anyone else on the team, I attended meetings, I never traveled or attended a fashion show, but I also never made a coffee. We would prefer to do only the interesting and funniest activities, but it's part of the game to accept the whole package and do even what seems boring in the beginning.

My hope is that by telling you these things and describing what you could experience in your first months inside the fashion industry, you'll keep going without taking things personally or thinking that the company is treating you differently from others because they don't consider you smart enough. Consider the internship period as a temporary process. And then you'll do many interesting and fun things even as an intern than bringing coffee. In the chapter dedicated to careers in fashion you can read what activities await you if you are about to start your next internship.

Most of fashion interns are in fact enthusiastic because they finally manage to get into the industry they have dreamed about and admired, so making some photocopies sometimes instead of organizing a closet, assisting a stylist on a photoshoot, or sending invitations for fashion events, is not such a bad compromise.

I would also like to point out something else that I believe is important to mention. Bringing some coffees and making photocopies is legitimate to an extent. Having been in this world for several years now, unfortunately I have also heard more severe stories than picking up your boss's laundry. Some interns have told me creepy stories about how the boss mistreated them and even threatened to ruin their career forever in this industry. Fortunately, these are rare cases, but I want to tell you that if you feel like you are in a toxic environment like this, you have to quit. Forget those who tell you that getting work is difficult and the fact that you have one is a miracle and that you should clench your teeth and go ahead with that job. When your boss insults you or, worse still, threatens you, it is not a miracle to be there, it is on the verge of absurdity and there is no reason in the world that you should stay. It doesn't matter how influential that person is in fashion, you don't have to accept such compromises. I'm shocked when I hear these stories and I do not understand how it is possible that such people exist. Respect must be on both sides; It shouldn't only be coming from you. If something similar ever happens to you feel free to email me! I had to mention this but don't want go too deep into this topic because I think that fashion is still a wonderful industry to work in with so much creativity and wonderful opportunities.

Let us return to fashion internships.

A popular time to do internships, especially among those who study because they are easy to juggle with schoolwork, is during the summer. Summer internships are the most famous in fashion and it is generally the time of year when you can find most internships.

Even if the city where you live is not a fashion capital like New York,

London, Milan, or Paris, and you feel discouraged because you feel left out of the fashion world and there are not as many internships opportunities in your town, you can always consider moving to a new city just for the summer. An internship abroad is gold on your resume; companies love this.

Summer internships usually last from one to three months and many students and recent graduates take advantage of this opportunity and this time of year to gain work experience and move to a new country and learn a new language as well. These experiences abroad don't just build your resume, they build you as a person. You get in touch with a new culture and a new language, and you live by yourself for the first time. They are excellent in terms of both professional and personal development, so if you have the opportunity, look for internships abroad.

If there is one thing I regret not doing when studying was to intern during the summer. But I wasn't aware of these opportunities in fashion at that time. So I'm writing this book to help all of you to not make my same mistakes and save precious time. If I could go back to my university years, I would definitely do an internship every summer, possibly one in every fashion capital.

Just by doing a summer internship every year when you are still in school you can build up a great dose of experience on your CV without too many sacrifices as you can focus on your studies throughout the rest of the year and find your next internship or job much easier and faster.

Planning your fashion internship

Whether you are studying or have recently graduated and you want to do an internship, it is always better if you can plan it in advance and not apply at the last minute, for many reasons.

First, because you have access to more opportunities and you will not have to "settle" only for the last internships available, having weeks or months to choose among the most interesting ones.

Secondly, because the sooner you can apply for a job offer, the better. A position could be closed at any moment. Despite this, take your time to work on your application. Applying without having carefully reread your CV or taking the time to write an oustanding cover letter is never a good idea. With these two documents you are introducing yourself to the company and playing your chances to get a job. You can't go wrong.

The third reason why you should plan your internship in advance is because you might want to consider the opportunity to intern abroad. Most of the fashion companies are located in the fashion capitals of Milan, London, New York, and Paris. If you do not live in one of these cities or if you want to have an experience abroad, you must plan it in advance to get all the necessary documents, secure an apartment, and figure out everything else that you need before going there.

The last reason is because if you plan an internship that you want to do in a couple of months, you have the time to save the money you need to move abroad (fashion capitals are expensive) and to know how

many months you can survive unpaid. If you have set money ₹
you can do the math and figure out if you can afford two months of
an unpaid internship and then look for another job, or combine your
internship with a secondary job in a coffee shop or work during the
weekend to make ends meet.

This is an example of a timeline that shows the times of year when
you should start considering an internship:

Summer Fashion Internships (June-August)	Start looking for them in January
Fall Fashion Internships (September/October/November)	Start looking for them in May
Spring Fashion Internships (March-May)	Start looking for them in October

Internships are the first building blocks of a successful career in
fashion. The more internships you can do the better. As I said, the
goal is to turn an internship into a full-time job.

14
WORKING DURING
FASHION WEEK

The weeks before and during fashion month represent the most intense days for fashion workers. It's that time of the year when the industry is ready to show to the world the result behind months and months of hard work. With the digital revolution and global events such as the 2020 pandemic, many brands have started using technology to introduce new ways of showing their collections to more and more people. But fashion shows are still the best way to introduce the new collections to the industry and consumers, and, according to some of the top fashion designers, they are here to stay, despite the industry's challenge during the pandemic, when brands were forced to cancel their fashion shows and bring them entirely online, and the innovations brought by technology.

Fashion weeks have been around since 1943, when the first one was held in New York with the purpose to give fashion buyers alternatives to French fashion during World War II. Haute couture shows have been held in Paris since 1945, when the Chambre Syndicale de la Haute Couture required couture houses to present a collection of at least thirty-five runs to the press. The more organized "semaine de la mode," that we know today was put together by the French Fashion Federation (Fédération Française de la Couture) in 1973. The first fashion weeks began in Milan in 1958 and London in 1984.

Fashion weeks were initially exclusively for fashion insiders, especially buyers and media. Since the first bloggers arrived in the front rows and above all with live streaming, fashion shows have become democratic and accessible to everyone.

However, while everyone can watch a fashion show at the same time as those present there in person, access to the physical event is still only for fashion insiders and influencers.

Being able to attend a fashion show live in person is a unique emotion. I have been lucky enough to attend fashion shows and for those who are passionate about fashion, the moment when the lights on the catwalk turn on and when the designer comes out to take their well-deserved applause, it is like goosebumps.

Unfortunately, access to a show is still not available even for purchase, even if some brands such as Balmain, who organized a show/concert in 2019, have experimented with this formula. So unless you work in the industry, you are an influencer, or you are willing to go to the guard at the entrance and beg them to let you in saying you'll stand in a corner, it is nearly impossible to gain access to the fashion shows.

That is, *unless you are part of one of the hundreds of people involved in the event.* If you are at the beginning of your career in fashion, you can be involved in these incredible events, not by just watching them online from your bedroom, but by being behind the scenes. A few people know that there is the possibility to work during fashion week and help backstage. To be honest, I didn't know about this opportunity when I was at the beginning of my career in fashion. Probably because I was not living in Milan before and so for me fashion week season was just watching my favorite shows on Vogue.com, live streaming and dreaming about being in the front row one day.

You can work as a volunteer during fashion week and help backstage. This is an experience that I recommend to anyone: students, graduates, and all those who are at the beginning of their career in fashion, no matter what fashion job they want to get later. Whether you want to work in design, pr, as a stylist, or in marketing, working backstage is an amazing experience not only for the chance to live and breathe a bit of the fashion industry from the inside, but you can promote it to prospective employers to get an internship and furthermore use it to grow your connections in the industry even if you don't have a job yet. Some people consider it a very stressful and useless experience where people will just "use" you, but to be honest if you love this industry and you want to be part of a fashion show this is your only way to get access to fashion week unless you already work in fashion or if you have friends that can get you inside.

Working as a fashion week volunteer can last from a single day to the entire fashion week, depending on how many shows you'll work on, but trust me that even working a couple of hours for a show will be rewarding.

It depends on the brand, but usually fashion week jobs include: dressing the models, setting up the locations, running errands, steaming garments, packing and unpacking clothes from one location to the other, welcoming guests ... Most of these jobs are very manual and include practical tasks, but this doesn't mean they are less important.

There are many small aspects that you don't think about that go into the production of a mere fifteen-minute show and your work is as precious as everyone else's. Can you imagine if there wasn't anyone to dress up the model with the second look? The show would be ruined! So the job of a volunteer is important and also very hard. Days start very early in the morning and end late at night and they are rarely paid, but considering that they last on average from one to three days, it's not a bad compromise as these experiences will teach you a lot.

So you might be wondering how and where to find fashion week jobs.

You could do research on Google for "fashion week jobs" in New York, Milan, Paris, or London. If you don't find anything, the best way to get a volunteer experience is to cold-email all the brands and pr agencies (we will talk soon about this cold email strategy and how to use it). Download the fashion week calendar even from past seasons from the official websites of each fashion week (LondonFashionWeek.com for London, www.cameramoda.it/ for Milan, parisfashionweek.fhcm.paris for Paris, and www.CFDA.com for New York), and email brands and pr agencies and tell them you'd like to help backstage during fashion week.

Don't just email the biggest brands but consider also new designers as well as those who don't show but who organized a presentation to show their collection. Every experience is valuable. Don't email two days before the show; the earlier you start contacting people the better. In November you can already reach out for the February round of fashion week. You'll get more chances of getting a job if you ask in advance, as these spots filled up quickly.

Once you've found an opportunity, make the most of it.
Keep focusing on doing a great job while you're there, but also speak to as many people as possible being careful to do it at the right time and not five minutes before showtime; make an excellent impression with everyone, from the other assistants and volunteers to the designer and any editors, stylists, and other figures you meet behind the scenes; get as many email contacts as possible so you can use them to send over your CV for an internship opportunity. As you can imagine, backstage, right before the show starts, things can get a bit crazy, chaotic, and sometimes dramatic, so be prepared for a good dose of stress and pressure behind the scenes of a fashion show. Don't let that intimidate you. Take notes when people tell you what your job duties are, and make sure to ask all of your questions in that moment instead of doing it five minutes before showtime. Don't be afraid to ask if something is not clear or if you think they might have missed something.
In order to do your best work and leave a good impression, you need to keep your stress under control and be sure you work quickly, especially when you have to change the look of your model before they go back to the runway. So if you know exactly what to do you won't feel so much pressure.

To recap:

Yes it's possible to work backstage during fashion week even if you are not employed by that brand. Brands work with volunteers just for this occasion.

Working as a volunteer is a great way to:

- Learn more about the behind the scenes of the fashion industry
- Have some experience to show to recruiters when you'll be looking for an internship
- Meet people in the industry and leverage those connections to get future jobs (don't be afraid to email these people after the show to ask for an internship).

I think there is something magical in this experience as volunteer. Even if you are going to be doing small tasks, you will proudly feel part of the show.

Working as a volunteer is just one of many experiences you can do even before your internship. In fact, this kind of experience enriches your CV, so you have something to show to future employers when you'll apply for internships. In the following chapters I'll also give you other example of experiences you can do if you want to add something on your CV before applying for internships.

15

THE POWER
OF WORD OF MOUTH and
NETWORKING FROM
0

One day I was in the office during my internship when I heard some managers talking about the need to hire someone new. One of them said: "I know someone who would be perfect for this job, I will ask her to send over the CV." You've probably already watched a scene like this on television or in the movies. Well, it really happens.

I already knew that getting to know someone in the industry would be crucial to my career and, in fact, when I was looking for my first fashion job, I always feared that not knowing anybody would be a problem for me. I knew that connections in the industry could introduce you to this world and help you find a job faster.

If internships are your ticket to the fashion industry, consider your network to be the previous step because it represents the most valuable career tool you will need at any stage of your career: from getting your first internship to all future career opportunities.

That conversation in the office confirmed everything.

So yes, it is true that getting to know fashion people helps you a LOT with your career.

Networking can seem like a very uncomfortable thing to do and you may think that it's only for extroverts and that as an introvert you will never be successful at building your own network.

But that's not the case.

Today, tools like LinkedIn and Instagram have broken down every barrier. You can connect with your favorite editors, stylists, designers, buyers, managers, interns... from anywhere in the world. The double advantage of these tools is that you can connect with literally anyone in the fashion industry and you can do it via a message which is ideal, even for the most introverted. You can already forget the fear of networking just by considering that you don't have to introduce yourself to people in person.

80% of the jobs and the best collaborations and projects in fashion are assigned by word of mouth.

It is thanks to your network that you will be able to learn about an upcoming opportunity at a specific company. And it is always your network that can help you find a new job or internship faster.

Many times fashion companies do not publish a job offer online because they will likely find someone within the circle of employees in the company. With so many people working in a fashion company, their pool of talent is already big enough that they've probably hired someone before the job even hits the job boards online and you can apply. So, you have to be in that circle. You need to have your own fashion network to have more opportunities. The more people you know, the more career opportunities you will have.

When you learn about a job opportunity, the first person you think of is your friend, the person you know and trust in their skills to the point of recommending them. You wouldn't propose someone who connected with you on LinkedIn and who you've never talked to.

Having lots of connections on LinkedIn will likely allow you to stay up-to-date with news and even job offers, but it won't help you in your career if you just leave them as connections and don't establish relationships with your contacts.

Networking doesn't mean adding as many people as possible on LinkedIn or following as many people on Instagram.

You need to establish a relationship. You need to put a strategy in place. As I've just mentioned, there is no point in having hundreds of LinkedIn connections and not interacting with anyone. It's not like when you meet a new friend randomly in a coffee shop. Networking is more strategic, you should not leave it to chance. When you connect with someone to network, you are usually thinking of people who can help you in your career. Which doesn't mean "using" people, otherwise you won't see results. It is very important that you build genuine relationships. In fact, I prefer to call your network: professional friendships.

You should never start a conversation by saying, "Hi, I'd like to work in your company, this is my resume." This is not networking, but more of a cold-application done the wrong way (we'll see it in the following chapters).

Wouldn't you be more willing to help someone who says:

"Hello, I found your LinkedIn profile / I read your interview on glamobserver.com / listened to your podcast interview and I really admire your career as an [editor, buyer…]. I am at the beginning of my career

in fashion, I would like to know more about this industry, and it would be a pleasure to talk to you because I have a lot of respect for your work. When do you have ten minutes for a quick phone call to answer a couple of questions about your fascinating career? If you prefer to reply by email I would be happy to send over some questions. I know you are busy so I will only take a few minutes of your time."

While both networking and spontaneous application seem to have the common goal of getting you a job opportunity, networking is much more. It's not just about reaching out to people to get a job, it's about building meaningful relationships with people, talking about a certain topic, and sometimes even finding a mentor.

Ideally you should cultivate these long-term relationships and don't forget about them. I am an introverted person too, so I want to share what helped and pushed me to meet more people. I know that networking is fundamental to anyone's career and business and that it is the foundation of all success. When you decide you want to be successful, you have to take into account having to do the hard things and getting out of your comfort zone. I can tell you that the best things always happen after months of hard work and it's never a straight road. So today I no longer wonder if I should send that message or that email, I just hit the send button and that's it. And you know what? In the end, it's not as bad as I thought. First of all because when you are networking online, you are "safe" on the other side of your laptop, so nothing can actually happen to you and secondly, I have learned to accept "no" and not let it bother or stop me. I just contact the next person. I interview fashion professionals for the website and the podcast so I have to contact strangers often (I actually feel like I know them since I follow them on social media, read their book, attended an event, read an interview ... but they have no idea who I am) to ask if they want to join me in a conversation and talk about their career in fashion.

I first had to face the hesitation of approaching people by introducing myself into their email inbox, and then the uncertainty of having to talk to them for 30-60 minutes if they accepted my interview request in English (not my native language). Everyone is insecure even when it doesn't seem like it, especially the first times we do something new, but that shouldn't be the reason you give up. I had so many reasons to give up: I'm introverted, I'm not very chatty, English is not my mother tongue. But would the alternative have been to give up everything just because of these fears? No way.

I remember I was twelve when the film *A Cinderella Story* with Hilary Duff came out and I watched it many times. A sentence from the film that has stuck with me and that I still remember today is:

"Don't let the fear of losing stop you from participating."

I repeat this to myself every time I have to do something that scares me.

Networking is a key part of anyone's career.

It has also helped me to consider that other people also want to build their network and meet new people, so you are doing them a favor too! Yes, you may think that right now no one wants to connect with you because you are not famous in fashion, you don't have a job and that therefore others are not interested in you because you have nothing to offer. But soon you will enter the fashion industry and work for some brands, and everyone knows that getting to know more people even from different companies is always useful. One day they will need your help too!

HOW TO NETWORK

Thankfully, you can build your network from scratch easily today due to the power of online connections and get in touch with anyone from all over the world, wherever you are: your favorite New York City fashion editor, the buyer who lives in London, the stylist who works in Milan…

Do not connect only with senior figures or those who have a public profile, also connect with fellow interns or assistants. It's easier to start conversations this way and it's more natural to create a real friendship since you are a similar age. There is also always something to learn from anyone's experiences and fellow interns can be a great source of support.

When it comes to building your network from scratch, you'll start by reaching out to strangers. This is completely normal and yes, you can send an email or a message to a stranger. This has become the new normal in communication since emails were introduced in the 1960s, and more recently, direct messages on social media.

The best way to connect with someone and break the ice is to show genuine interest in someone's career. Ideally you will connect with people who today have your dream job and work in your favorite companies, but you can also diversify and connect with other professionals from different departments.

If you want to become a designer, you will surely be interested in wanting to learn more about other designers' careers. When you have a genuine interest in someone's career, it's easier and more spontaneous to ask the right questions.

Before connecting with someone, do some research online so that you can personalize your message even more and show real interest—you can compliment them on a recent role change, an interview, or anything you can find online to prove that you did your research. Not everyone working in fashion is in the spotlight, so you might want to get in touch with the trend forecaster who has never released any interviews, or been mentioned in any articles. Your research work here is on LinkedIn: learn about their career path: what they studied, their first job... so you can make specific references when you contact them.

In order to see results, networking should be like a part-time job for you.

You need to network on a consistent basis.

The best way to do this is to create a sheet with a list of people you want to interact with. Start an Excel spreadsheet and set a goal of reaching 3-5 fashion professionals per week.

Head over to www.glamobserver.com/book to download a free Excel sheet to boost your networking strategy.

WHERE TO NETWORK

Online networking via email, LinkedIn, or Instagram is fantastic, but if you can combine it with offline connection, even better.

While online networking is a strategy that works and is especially useful for networking with people who don't live in your city and for breaking the ice for the first time, your offline connections are stronger. As you can probably imagine, the type of relationship you build with someone you meet in person is totally different than the type of relationship you build with someone through emails.

My advice is therefore to bring some of your connections that you have initiated online, offline, by inviting someone for a coffee for example.

Another great way to build offline connections is to attend fashion events. Over the years I have organized fashion panels to encourage offline connections within the community. Look for a fashion event on sites such as Eventbrite in your city or in another fashion capital, that you could combine in a personal trip.

The more events you can attend, the better.

When you go to these events, you should set a goal to talk to at least 3-4 people and leave with their email contacts. Start by greeting the person sitting next to you, introduce yourself and continue the conversation by asking if this is the first time they have attended such an event, if they like it, why they are attending, what they do, and then the conversation will continue naturally. A smile or a compliment on a dress can also be a fun and efficient conversation starter. During the talks, ask questions, so that eventually people come to you intrigued by what you asked.

· · · · · · · · · · · · · · · · · · ·

Even once you've found your job, you shouldn't stop networking. Your network is not only useful at the beginning of your career, but also later for your future role and career opportunities, when you might need advice or information pertaining to your job. While you'll likely network less and meet people organically at your job, meeting people outside of your office is something you should never stop doing. At that point in your career, it's not just you trying to get something out of people but rather a dual-sided relationship where you can also offer support. Depending on the stage of your career, you will network with different people. You may find yourself at a point where you are indecisive with your career and therefore want to connect with someone who can guide you and help you with personal development.

I'm sure you don't want to do all this hard work and then lose your connections. You should divide your time by building new relationships and cultivating the ones you have built. Keep in touch with your former boss or colleagues to stay fresh in their minds so they remember you if they have an exciting opportunity that could be great for you. Email them from time to time, congratulate them when they post about their new job on LinkedIn, reply to their IG story, if you see exciting news about the company, send your congratulations.

Remember to help others, whether they are fellow interns, assistants, stylists, editors ... be kind to everyone, help them with sincerity so you will be more confident to ask for help in return when you need it. It doesn't matter if you are still at the beginning of your career, you always have something to give, there is always something that you know and that you take for granted, that others might not know. Maybe it is an Excel function, or how to use a social media feature ... or simply even by reading this book you have, I hope, learned something useful that you could pass on to someone else.

Start networking today and never stop.

16

SOCIAL MEDIA
IS THE NEW RESUME

Before personal websites, LinkedIn, and Instagram, the only way for companies to evaluate a candidate was by looking at a sheet of paper: the resume.

With social media everything has changed. While it is true that they have exposed the fashion industry to many more people making it even more competitive, on the other hand you can exploit them to your advantage. Nowadays as soon as a recruiter receives an application, one of the first things they do is search for their name online. From there they begin to visit LinkedIn profiles, photos on Facebook, and Instagram accounts.

If it sounds creepy, the good news is that you can give recruiters a chance to get to know you better and use these tools to your advantage.

Most of the times, the problem with the resume lies in the fact that it is difficult to express one's skills through a sheet of paper. It is unfair that a company decides whether or not you are good for the job without giving you the opportunity to prove what you are worth. These online tools give us the opportunity to add videos, photos, texts, and other material to the job application, providing more information about you to the company that may help to convince them to invite you for a job interview.

Demonstrating your skills and competences directly rather than letting a company classify you based on just a resume is the best way to get a job in fashion.

Social media is a great tool for showing what you know and what you can do. If they were initially born as an online space to share everyday life moments, social media soon became a powerful business tool now used by all brands to reach a larger audience than traditional advertising.

Just as companies leverage social media to reach more consumers, so you should too for your career. Today recruiters and your future bosses are online and they are your target just as consumers are for brands. Brands show a product with the aim of convincing a consumer to purchase; you show your skills with the aim of intriguing the recruiter who will invite you to an interview, or showing your future boss that you are the right person for that job.

If up until now you have only used social media to get in touch with friends and follow your favorite influencers, know that you can also be social with professionals in the fashion sector and get much more out of it than just a travel or outfit idea.

Social media has become the new resume.

The company may be impressed by how you communicate on Instagram, or how you built your website, from an article you published on your blog, from a comment you left on LinkedIn, from the websites and books you read and share. If you know how to take advantage of social media, it can give you many advantages in your career.

Leah Chernikoff, former Digital Director at *Elle*, said she hired writers from comments found in *Elle*'s Instagram posts. A Break into the Fashion Industry student found a job as an assistant stylist by sending a DM on Instagram!

The possibilities are truly endless. Think about how many people you can reach online even from the other side of the world.

Obviously, social networks are a double-edged sword. Offensive or inappropriate photos and posts could work to your disadvantage, which is why, even before you decide to start applying for jobs, make sure you clean up your profiles and start using them logically. This does not mean only publishing perfect photos or posting only content related to your work. Online you are building your personal branding. Think about how you want the company to perceive you and adjust your posts accordingly. If you want the company to think that you are interested in the world of fashion, that you like to travel, that you are sociable, kind, professional, and take pilates classes, then post content that shows these passions and characteristics.

Everything outside of work says more about your personality and how you spend your free time, so it's not necessary to post just about fashion and your career.

Each social network should be used differently based on its purpose. LinkedIn is used exclusively for professional purposes and for your career, so don't post photos of your travels, parties, or jokes with your friends. On Instagram you can show more of a range and reveal personality traits that a LinkedIn profile does not show.

A key benefit of social media is that it is two-sided. You're not the only one who is looking for contacts and job opportunities, but you can be found by the right people. Companies scout on social media. Wouldn't it be great if job offers came to you? If your social media profiles are on point, you may receive a job interview request even without having sent your application (you may also already have a job and be contacted by a company that found you online). Getting discovered by the right people such as recruiters, managers, editors, stylists is always useful throughout your career, but especially when you are on a job hunt. Which means that when you are actively looking for a new job or internship you should spend more time leveraging them. Companies search by keywords, and social media works like a search engine (think about Google), so to make your profile pop up in the search results, you need to set up your profile correctly and post content with the right hashtags such as:

#stylist #photoshoot #fashionarticle #fashioneditor

#fashionwriter #fashionphotographer #fashionbuyer
#fashionpr

If you want to become a stylist you will obviously have to show your styling skills; if you want to become a photographer you will publish your shots, if you want to become a designer your sketches, and so on. Unless you want to become an influencer, there is no need to update your profiles every day several times a day, but you should still keep them active and, above all, you should connect every day to interact with the posts that fashion industry professionals have published on LinkedIn and Instagram to engage with them.

Do you remember the networking chapter you just read?

As mentioned in that chapter, social media is the ideal place to network and then quickly expand your knowledge in the sector with anyone from anywhere in the world. You can start from scratch and within an hour be connected with ten fashion industry professionals or more from the comfort of your home. If you are thinking that all this is too much and you would like to prevent people from forming an opinion of you from your online presence, know that not being present on any social network can make companies suspicious and, according to a survey, some recruiters reject people who do not have any social presence. So social media is essential for building your personal brand, showing your skills, networking, and getting a job. The two most powerful social media platforms for your career are LinkedIn and Instagram.

LINKEDIN

LinkedIn is the ultimate career social media platform. It is the only social network developed exclusively for professional use and, unlike the others, is not meant for sharing information about your personal life.

If you don't have a LinkedIn profile yet, create one today. Before using LinkedIn for anything you need to set up a professional profile.

Fill in as much information as possible. With LinkedIn, the more complete the profile, the more it will appear when someone is searching online, therefore:

• Add the right keywords in your bio, skills, and when describing your previous experiences. As we will see later with your resume, even on LinkedIn you should use a short description or bullet points to give more information about your previous work experience especially if it is in line with the job you would like to get.

• Add a professional photo taken from the shoulders up. Profiles with photos appear in more searches. I never accept connection requests from those who don't have a profile photo.

• Add links to your website / portfolio

• Upload your portfolio or any relevant documents (articles you wrote, a PDF you created for a brand ...)

• Your email address so that you can easily be contacted by email and not just through messages via the platform.

Once you've set up your profile, you can start using LinkedIn for its most useful purpose: expanding your network and connecting with industry professionals. You have to connect with people you know (students from your course, colleagues and former colleagues), and people you would like to know: those who work in the companies where you would like to apply, people in the industry that you admire, and those with whom you would like to have an informational interview (more about this in the next chapters).

Super important: every time you connect with someone on LinkedIn that you don't know, don't send a simple connection request but fill out the part of the note that LinkedIn allows you to send as a message along with your connection request. Ideally you should explain why you would like to add them to your network, such as saying you admire their career. With this simple message, many more people will accept your connection request.

With the many LinkedIn connection requests I get daily I tend to accept more easily those who add a personal note. Remember that what is important isn't the number of connections you have, but the quality of those connections. On LinkedIn you will receive several connection requests from people who have nothing to do with the fashion industry, so don't feel obliged to add people to your network who are not useful to your career. You also don't want to have your LinkedIn feed filled with articles on topics you don't care about and miss important updates from connections that matter. So remember to connect with and accept only the right people.

LinkedIn is not just a social media, so its advantages don't stop at showing your skills and connecting with professionals in the sector. One of its important features is the ability to search for job offers.

Therefore, LinkedIn is your best career ally, where in one place you can connect with those who work in fashion and stay up-to-date on the latest job openings posted. You can search for job offers by keywords: "fashion", "fashion internship", "fashion buyer", "stylist", "summer internship", and filter them by years of experience required, location, etc.

Many fashion industry professionals share on LinkedIn when they are looking for someone to join their team, so in addition to the job offers section of the platform, keep an eye on the updates posted by those who work in fashion. That's why connecting at least once a day on LinkedIn is useful to stay up-to-date on any offers and industry news.

TIP: Download the app on your smartphone so you can use LinkedIn faster and more frequently.

While on Facebook and Instagram people share a *Vogue* article about the latest lipstick to buy, the posts that people share on LinkedIn concern the business side of fashion. So it's the perfect way to stay up-to-date with what's going on in the industry: a new creative director, sustainability issues, a new industry report ...

Companies also have pages on LinkedIn, more or less like on Facebook, where they post content relating to job offers and career updates such as interviews of those who work there, articles to understand more about what it means to work at that company, learn about new CEO and marketing director appointments, internship programs and other interesting news. In addition to setting your profile with keywords to appear in searches, another way to be found on LinkedIn is to be active by commenting or replying to content. Someone might land on your profile from a comment you left under an editor/stylist/buyer/publicist 's post.

Don't just use LinkedIn to collect information, but share useful content too:

• Articles you've read about the sector published by sites such as Business of Fashion, WWD, Vogue, Glam Observer;) that show your interest in the topic.

• An article you wrote, an editorial where you were the assistant on set, your updated portfolio, a fashion photo you took, the new cover or an update of the magazine or company you work for

• Your career goals

LinkedIn is also useful when you need to do your research and understand who works where, especially when you want to do a self-application (more about this tool in the next chapters) and you need to know who the editor, stylist, merchandiser, or recruiter of that company is so you can reach out to them directly.

It's very useful to do some research on LinkedIn even before the job interview to understand who will be your boss, what they studied, where they were working, as well as information about the team you'll be working with. You can also understand who a company tends to hire: if only women work there, if everyone is under 30, how diverse and international it is.

INSTAGRAM

If LinkedIn is the professional social media platform and there is no doubt that it should be used exclusively for your career, Instagram was created to share moments of your personal life, so knowing how to use it for your career could be a bit vague, but necessary.

These days it's no longer used for personal purposes only, because whether you like it or not, whoever might hire you will look at your profile first.

There are those who decide to have two separate profiles:
• a private one for personal use only
• a second one used for professional content, that acts as a portfolio and to build the personal brand, where fashion and career related content is shared

And there are those who decide to have only one public profile and mix personal life with professional content: so they publish both the family trip to New York and the behind-the-scenes of a photo shoot, or a screenshot of an article published.

You should choose which option is the best for you according to how you use your personal profile. Remember that if the profile is public you should still avoid posting personal photos that are not appropriate.

Once you have decided which option to go with, you have to set up correctly your profile, the one that is public.

Set up your bio, use your name and surname as your username, add the link to your portfolio or website or LinkedIn profile, and don't forget to enter your professional email address so that people can easily get in touch.

Remember that the number of followers doesn't matter unless you want to become an influencer. So don't fixate on having to post the right content to increase your followers, but remember that the goal is to reach the right people so use the right hashtags to get discovered by the one person that might change your career.
Of course, if you want to work as a social media manager, having more followers is an asset that shows your ability to grow followers but even in this case it is not necessary to have a high number of followers. There are many social media managers of major brands and magazines who do not have thousands of followers on Instagram.

Once you've set up your profile, it's time to start following fashion industry professionals. Start following a bit of everything and everyone to be updated on various aspects of the fashion industry: brand accounts, magazines, editors, buyers, PR, agencies, showrooms ... Obviously, if you use Instagram to network, you have to be selective about who to follow depending on what you need at that time.
When I was at the beginning of my career in fashion, I didn't know all the people who worked in this industry. Sure, I knew

the most popular figures such as Anna Wintour or Donatella Versace, but not all stylists, buyers, or publicists. It has taken me years to build a comprehensive list of fashion industry professionals, that's why to save time and since it is vital to follow those who work in fashion on Instagram, I have included in my online course Break into the Fashion Industry a list of over 100 people with links to their Instagram profiles divided between stylists, editors, managers, designers, and CEOs.

There are various reasons why you should follow those who work in fashion on Instagram:

1. To learn more about their work and what goes on behind the scenes of fashion

Everyone shares at least a couple of Instagram stories every week. And fashion professionals are no exception. If you are a stylist, buyer, journalist, or publicist and you spend most of your weekly hours working, your stories can't help but show some of the behind-the-scenes moments of your working days and the fashion industry in general. So following those who work in fashion will allow you to take a look at the offices of fashion companies and the activities of those who work there. Fashion professionals also attend industry events, most of which are exclusive and closed to the public, but you can still get an inside look by looking at their stories and posts wherever you are. Sometimes those who work in fashion also do Q&A sessions on Instagram, so you can take the opportunity to ask your questions related to their career and ask for some advice.

2. Get updates on the latest job opportunities

Whether they work at a fashion company, in an agency or magazine, or for themselves (stylists, photographers, freelancers, designers), fashion professionals use Instagram also to promote job offers. I often share screenshots of jobs posted by industry professionals on their Instagram profiles. Most of the time when they post a new job or internship they also add their personal email, so you can proceed with an email application rather than the standard online application, which you will see in the next chapters is much more effective when it comes to standing out in this competitive industry.

3. The more you know, the more successful you will be in getting the job or internship

The more personalized your application (CV, cover letter, emails), the better the chances of getting the job. The same goes for the job interview; the more you know the person in front of you, the more successful you will be. Fashion professionals share not only their professional life on Instagram, but also their private life and their opinions on specific issues in society and fashion such as sustainability, inclusivity, etc ... It is extremely important to know what they think about different topics and what their preferences are in order to know what to say or not to say in an email or during the job interview. The more you know, the more successful you will be in getting the job or internship.

4. Expand your network (easily)

The most obvious reason is that the more people you follow on Instagram, the more chances you have of bonding with some of them and establishing a solid and genuine relationship that will help you with your fashion career in your early days and also later on when you want to find a new job. Word of mouth is the best way to get a job in fashion and Instagram is the easiest way to build relationships with anyone from anywhere in the world. You have the opportunity to connect with anyone even from the other side of the world that you would not have otherwise. Do you know of another way to connect with the editor in chief of *Harper's Bazaar* if you don't work at that company?

If the first step is to start following those who work in fashion, the second step, which is even more important, is to start interacting. Remember that what's important isn't the number of connections you have on LinkedIn or the people you follow on Instagram. To get benefits and career opportunities it is not necessary to simply follow more people but to interact and build true relationships.

So if the first step is obviously to follow their accounts, the next one is to start interacting so that they become familiar with your profile and name. Start liking (you can turn on the update notification so you don't miss their latest posts) and leaving comments. In this case, of course, I do not mean a simple emoticon or something obvious that only serves to receive some visits from those who are commenting on that post as well. If you want results, you have to leave meaningful comments in which, for example, you express your opinion and allows others to understand your point of view, personality, and find something in you that convinces them not just to visit your profile, but to contact you to establish a relationship.

Commenting is the most effective way to be discovered by people and to establish relationships. From a comment comes a follow, which can be turned into a series of direct messages leading up to an email, call, and maybe a meeting in person. After a couple of weeks of interacting with the content publicly, it's time to move on to private messages. Send a DM or an email starting with a career compliment or a role update, or an interview you read.

I use this trick below to keep track of the people I want to establish relationships with on Instagram. Every time I find a profile that interests me, I save one of their posts in the Instagram collections. I love that Instagram has a function that allows you to save posts and group them into different collections. I have a collection for stylists, editors, CEOs ... I save them each time I'm on Instagram and I find someone interesting. Then one day a week I go back to my collections and try to interact with them! A simple way to create connections spontaneously and on a costistent base.

Using LinkedIn and Instagram is one of the unconventional strategies for getting a job today. You can interact with recruiters, editors, stylists, and all kinds of fashion professionals and get noticed before, after, or during your application process and even your job interview! More and more people today are noticed and get jobs and opportunities for collaborations through social media, so don't waste any more time and start using these platforms for your career right away.

17

FINDING A JOB EVEN WHEN YOU THINK THERE ISN'T ONE

In the standard job application process, everyone generally says to go to different websites that publish job vacancies, look at the list of jobs, and repeat day after day after until you find a job that suits you and apply.

Waiting for your favorite company to post the right job opening online could take months.

That's why, after reading these pages, you will no longer wait for your favorite company to post a job offer, but you will be the one to introduce yourself and send a cold email, doing a spontaneous application.

This is my absolute favorite strategy also because over the years, I have seen it bringing concrete results to everyone that has applied it correctly.

The advantages of sending cold emails are many:

1. The brand may have a position open or one that will open shortly but has not yet been posted online. Your email would then arrive at just the right time, beating everyone else to the punch.

2. Fashion is a very competitive industry. Going only through the online application process means trying to get noticed among around 500 candidates simply by leveraging your extraordinary CV and cover letter. Cold emails are more direct and arrive in the inbox of the recruiter or person you would like to work with and have a greater chance of being noticed.

3. Unlike a standard online application, with emails you can follow up in case you have not received a response. We said previously that following up is likely your key to success in everything and it should become a habit to do every time you send an email. When you apply for a job online, you cannot apply again so that your profile rises above all the candidates. But an email can come back to the top an inbox if you follow up, thus doubling the chances that the person you want to reach sees your application.

4. It is an unconventional strategy and therefore it is a great way to get noticed and show your spirit of initiative and proactivity that companies appreciate. With this strategy you show that you have something extra than all other candidates, even compared to those who have a CV with more experience than yours. As I said before, companies today are used to receiving CVs with a list of prestigious names of companies and universities, so they look for that extra something in candidates, which you will surely show by sending an email rather than following the conventional application process.

Cold emailing works with all companies, both the most prestigious ones and startups, agencies as well as magazines, but it is also useful when you want to work with people. For example, when you want to assist a stylist, photographer, or editor, or help out on a photo shoot, during events, or backstage during a fashion week. Sending a cold email is almost the only way to get these kinds of job opportunities because generally, they are rarely posted on job boards online.

Every time you say: "I've been looking for weeks but I can't find an internship or job opportunities," sending a cold email is the answer. Especially due to the recent challenging times of the pandemic that the number of job vacancies posted has dropped significantly. The first thing you need to do to apply this strategy is obviously to make a list of your favorite companies you would like to work for. If they don't have published on their careers page or other websites, a job that interests you or is right for you, get ready to send your cold email.

Some companies allow people to send a spontaneous application from their Work with us/Career page, in this case it is right to go through there to show that you have done your research.

Once you have identified the company you want to cold email, you have to find the right person to reach out to. It's very important that you send the email to the specific person you want to reach out and not using a generic email risking to make a hole in the water by contacting another team or someone who is not interested in your email. A cold email strategy works as long as you reach out to the right person.

When you have the email contact of the person you want to reach out to, it's time to write a powerful email that impresses the hiring manager or whoever you are reaching out. You must be professional, write a short and concise description of yourself, and attach your CV to the email. You have to "sell yourself" to the company by highlighting your best skills and how they will be useful for the company, referring also to the goals achieved during previous experiences. If you want to cold email for an internship, you can leverage your studies and desire to gain experience working at your favorite brand or with your favorite people by showing how passionate and hard working you are.

• • • • • • • • • • • • • • • • • • •

Using unconventional strategies is necessary in fashion. Most of the time the problem with fashion job applications is that they don't even get noticed due to the large number of those received. So often the problem is not that your profile is not suitable for that position, but rather that your CV may not even reach the person concerned. Sending an email, on the other hand, is the most direct way to get noticed by someone.

18

THE INFORMATIONAL
INTERVIEW

Together with the cold email strategy, the informational interview is a tool that will make a difference in your career in fashion. We have already talked about it and given some details in the chapter "The myth of the dream job."

What is an informational interview?
The informational interview is a meeting with a fashion industry professional that can be done in person, online, or via phone call, in which you ask questions regarding their career and role for the purpose of collecting information. The goal isn't in fact to share this information in a press interview or somewhere else. It's a private conversation with someone who works in fashion so that you can gain a better understanding of their job and

the industry, what it's like working at that company, and maybe even ask for some specific advice and recommendations before applying for a job.

Not everyone knows people who work in fashion. When I started thinking about wanting to work in this sector, I didn't know anyone who worked in fashion so I really missed being able to talk to someone about what it meant to work in fashion, what goes on in the office, what the industry truths are, and last but not least, what it takes to start a career.

If I had known about the informational interview, I would certainly have taken advantage of it immediately by dividing my hundreds of questions, doubts, and curiosities among fashion people.

Through the informational interview you can talk to anyone who works in fashion. Of course, Anna Wintour probably won't be available, but you can reach out to stylists, editors, publicists, buyers, e-commerce managers, those who work in a showroom, in an agency, in a large company, or a startup from anywhere in the world.

Who to contact will obviously depend on the type of information you need. You can find out what it means to work at MyTheresa in London, at Gucci in Italy or in their New York offices, working with secondhand at Vestiarie Collective, at a startup like Tagwalk, at *Vogue Italia*, British *Vogue*, or anywhere else in the world.

The benefits of having conversations with those who work in fashion are mainly three:

1. to collect information and understand more about a career or company as we have just said
2. to establish relationships
3. and lastly, to get a job

Let's give more details on the first one:

1.Collecting information

The informational interview is very useful to understand if you are really interested in a career option and especially if it is truly as great as you expected.

With the informational interview you ask questions such as:

What does your typical workday look like? What are your main activities? What do you like most about this job and what do you like least?

If you want to get a job that involves travel, you might want to ask how often they travel and where. If you want to attend fashion shows you might ask if going to fashion weeks is part of their job.

If you hate the idea of working with Excel all day, you might ask how many hours a day that person with your dream job now spends on Excel.

Let's say you want to work as a stylist. Through the informational interview you want to better understand what the key activities of a stylist are and how much time they spend on each activity to understand if it's really the job for you. So you look for stylists on Instagram or LinkedIn and contact them.

Each career in fashion has its own nuances so try to find at least a couple of people who work in different realities.

The stylist who works for a brand will surely have to deal with different responsibilities than stylists who work freelance, those who work on magazine editorials, those who work in e-commerce, and those who work with celebrities.

There are different shades of a role in all departments and types of companies in fashion.

The job of someone who works in PR in a brand is different from who works in PR at an agency that manages multiple brands.

Such as a Gucci buyer could take care of different things than a buyer who works at Burberry, but the same as the merchandiser there.

So when you want to learn more about a career, look for people who work in different business realities to learn more about the various facets of this profession and understand which path you prefer: agency vs company, retail vs e-commerce, iconic brand vs startup.

Remember that each person has a different opinion on different activities. Someone might tell you that they don't like their job because it is too stressful to go back and forth between one city and another, while for you the idea of traveling every week sounds fantastic. Someone else might tell you they didn't feel comfortable at a job because they were mainly doing an activity that you are interested in. Others may seem super enthusiastic about their work, but you don't like the idea of spending all day on your laptop. Collect information but always evaluate it according to your needs, passions, and the lifestyle you would like to have. Don't get swayed, stick to your opinions.

Don't just contact those in senior positions, but also fellow interns or assistants. It is interesting to understand which activities you will be involved with personally as an intern rather than just understanding the dynamics of a more senior role that you will reach in a few years. If you want to work as a PR intern, try asking several people who have been interns recently. Each company handles responsibilities differently. Maybe at company X the PR intern was involved only in press reviews, at company Y they supported the organization of events, at company Z they managed samples to be sent to magazines, stylists, and influencers. Especially when you have to cold email companies and people where you have the possibility to choose who to reach out to, the more you know about a role and a company, the more you can select, exclude, or consider companies to get in touch with. You can also request an informational interview with someone who used to work at a company that interests you, but no longer works there. The fact that they work for a different company now makes it easier for them to be more open about giving you information.

When requesting an informational interview, think carefully about the questions you want to ask. Obviously you will not be able to ask 100 questions and above all you will have to respect the agreed upon time for a call or a meeting in person (tip: to have a better chance of getting a positive response, ask to meet up at the cafe near their office rather than asking the person to meet you on the other side of the city). Before writing the questions you want to ask, do some research online to avoid asking about things you can find on Google or on their Linkedin profile and save your valuable and limited questions for things you want to know that you can't find anywhere.

Many times my Break into the Fashion Industry students tell me that after finishing the course the problem is no longer how to connect with someone, or where to find their email address or what to write in these emails and messages, but now that they have the tools, they are afraid to annoy them.

But the truth is, if you're nice and polite, you don't follow up the next day, and if you ask a few questions and not an endless list, you won't bother anyone. Yes, there are people who are not that willing to cooperate and probably won't reply to your emails, but that is nothing to worry about. The worst that can happen is that someone says they don't want to share this information, or they don't respond at all. But there are many wonderful people in fashion willing to help you. So even if one in ten people respond to your email, you have something valuable in your hands.

2.Build connections

Networking by starting with an informational interview is the simplest and most genuine way to establish connections. When you contact someone whose career interests you, asking questions and finding topic to discuss will be much easier.

So you can build a connection starting with an informational interview and then cultivate it over time.

3.Find work

The initial goal of an informational interview should never be to ask for a job. If you go straight to the point and attach your CV we are no longer talking about informational interview but a cold email/self-application. You have to learn to separate the two strategies and know how and with who to use one or the other. The informational interview is more of a long-term strategy than a short-term one like a cold email.

After a fifteen-minute informational interview over a coffee or a phone call, continue to cultivate the relationship. If you see that the person is collaborative and available you can ask them to keep you in mind for any job opportunities in their own company. You can also ask them if it's okay if you keep in touch if it makes you feel more comfortable. In the end, you will always contact people who work in the company where you would like to work, who do the job you would like to get, so they know that if you are interested in their career, it is because you would like to do something similar. So always be kind and respect whoever is in front of you or on the other side of the screen. The person you decide to contact for the informational interview must understand that you are truly interested in their career and that you admire them. If done well, an informational interview could bring you a job offer. The person you have an informational interview with might be impressed by your profile and ask you to work for them or recommend you to the hiring manager even after a couple of months.

Not everyone will accept your request for an informational interview; that's normal. Some people are busy, others can't discuss work due to company policy, others just aren't that open to collaboration ... but remember that just a few contacts can make a difference. So if you don't hear back from the first eight people you reached out to, just keep going and reach out to the next eight.

19

BUILDING A RESUME
WHEN YOU DON'T
HAVE EXPERIENCE

So far we've seen some unconventional application strategies to get noticed when applying for a job in fashion. If you ever attended one of my free webinars you might be familiar with one or some of them. If you have never attended a webinar with me visit _www.glamobserver.com/book_ where you'll find more resources. Although it is necessary to think about how to stand out with a creative application, the classic document such as the resume remains indispensable regardless of the application strategy you chose. This document is still part of the old standard job application process that is here to stay.

Just because you sent an email to a recruiter and surprised them by arriving directly in their inbox does not automatically mean a guaranteed invitation to a job interview. Whoever receives your application will first evaluate the documents you have attached. If your CV, cover letter or portfolio are not set up correctly, no unconventional strategy will work as it should.

Your resume represents your first contact with the company, and is like your business card, so everything must be perfect. The company does not know you. The way you create and set up this document says a lot about you. Not only the content, but the font and layout you choose for your CV show personal characteristics that the company pays attention to as much as the content.

It takes a recruiter about three seconds to decide if your resume will end up on their list of those to consider or those rejected.

If the structure is unclear and not well done, you will end up on the pile of discarded ones regardless.

You may be the perfect person for the job, have studied at the best schools, have work experience and all the required skills, but if your resume is not clear, or worse, has grammatical mistakes or typos and it is not easy to distinguish the various information, the company will probably discard it without having read it through. Don't sabotage your application by paying little attention to writing your CV.

A CV that is poorly-structured or has typos and grammatical mistakes is seen by companies as a sign that you didn't pay much attention to your application and therefore they assume you are not that interested in getting the job, and secondly, that you might make these kinds of mistakes if you're hired for the job.

If you want to set up it correctly, this is how your CV should appear:

• Clear and streamlined structure. The recruiter in three seconds must be able to understand where to find the section related to your experiences, what you studied, and your skills.

• One page only. There is no need to fill up multiple sheets. You should add the description of your previous experiences to give an idea of your responsibilities, but it's enough to organize them in bullet points with 3-4 activities per experience.

• PDF format. Whatever program you use to create your CV— Word, Photoshop, or other, remember to save it as a PDF and do not send other formats to the company. Ideally you should save the file by naming it: name.surname.CV.PDF. In 90% of cases you will send your resume online so you just need the file, but print a few copies when you know you might meet someone, such as when you attend an event. Today the best way is to ask for the email contact first and send your digital CV.

• Do not forget to include your e-mail and telephone contacts.

• Customize! <u>It is essential that your CV contains the keywords of the job offer and that it is absolutely personalized for that company.</u> Perhaps you are familiar with the concept of customizing a cover letter and you haven't thought it necessary to apply it to your resume as well. But it is very important to tweak your CV every time you apply for a new job offer. Some companies, especially large ones that receive thousands of resumes, use an ATS (Applicant Tracking System) that scans resumes and divides them based on keywords. If your CV does not contain the keywords for that position and the structure is not clear, the recruiter may never read yours because the system has rejected it.

You should therefore have a folder on your desktop for each brand and position and all the different versions of your CV. To fit your resume to the company, read the job description carefully and highlight the keywords. What is the company looking for? Someone who organizes the closet? Someone who writes three articles a day? What skills are they looking for? Someone who can work with Photoshop, Fashion Monitor, Launchmetrics? An organized, motivated person with a wide knowledge of the industry and the various fashion magazines? Identify the keywords you find both in the activity list of the job description and in the part dedicated to the requirements, and make sure to have them on your CV. Change the order of skills and descriptions, and add, remove, or replace experiences and details that are relevant to that offer. It is not necessary to add experiences that are not applicable to the job you are applying for. Put yourself for a moment in the role of the recruiter and make sure that your CV matches exactly the job offer request. When you are at the beginning of your career, it is normal to have a rather empty CV.

You don't have to come up with who knows what to add content to your resume. Eventually, when you are starting out you will mostly use it to apply for internships, which typically do not require previous work experience. In this case, in fact, it is better to play with the cover letter and make it strong, explaining how passionate you are and that you are ready to work hard to finally enter the company of your dreams. We will talk about this shortly.

However, I want to list some experiences that can enrich your CV to have more chances to get an internship.

In the chapter dedicated to internships we talked about how they represent your way to enter the fashion industry.

With so many applicants, it may happen that although the company does not require previous experience in the internship listing, it still receives applications from people who have some previous experience.

"The company told me they didn't choose me because they preferred someone with more experience. It is unfair for them to expect someone to already have experience for an internship."

I know. You might think, how can I ever get an internship if there will always be someone who has even just a couple of months more experience? Trust me, you can do it. Using an unconventional strategy such as the ones we talked about in previous chapters could impress the company more than a job experience. Never get discouraged by a list of requirements or thinking that there will always be someone with more experience and qualifications, but apply for any internship that interests you, keeping in mind ways to impress the company.

We said that the person who gets the job or internship is not the one who can necessarily do the job better, but the one who knows how to get hired. And this is what unconventional strategies are for, so use them.

In this chapter I want to give you some ideas of how to make your CV interesting in the eyes of companies, so you can get your first internship just by adding some simple experiences related to fashion.

Working backstage during fashion week

We have already talked about volunteer work during fashion week. Don't forget about this experience that you can do even before your first internship.

Assistant for a Photo Shoot

An extra hand is always needed on the set of a fashion photo shoot and this is also one of those jobs that can be obtained when you have no experience yet. Write to stylists, photographers,

PR, and fashion brands and tell them that you'd like to help them with anything they need help with for that day on set: dressing the models, ironing clothes, bringing coffee, sewing buttons, cleaning shoes, unpacking and packing clothes, helping the makeup artist or hair stylist. Show that you are willing to do anything necessary and don't ask to be paid (those tens of euros you would get for that day won't change your life and people will be more willing to let you come if you do it without asking for a fee). Days like these on a set will teach you a lot, they will introduce you to many people who may call you for other shoots and above all, you can start adding experiences to your resume.

Sales Assistant

Don't underestimate a sales assistant job. Even if your end goal is not to work in a store, for some corporate roles related to retail, you must first have in-store experience. One day a Louis Vuitton manager told me they spend months in the store on a rotation basis because the company thinks it is the best way to get to know the customer and therefore develop new strategies. Some companies ask for an experience in retail even when it comes to internships in buying and merchandising. This is a job that is easy to find part-time, so it is perfect to manage while studying.

Start your own blog or write for other publications

Start your own fashion blog, or write for an online or local magazine or even your school publication. Writing is not only essential if you want to start a career as an editor or fashion journalist, but it is also beneficial for other careers because it's a way to show your level of knowledge in the sector. Writing about fashion is not just about sharing the latest trends and suggesting what to wear. You could write about marketing, PR, sustainability ...

You never know who might read your articles. Choose a topic that is related to the department in which you would like to get your internship so that you can show your future boss that you know about that topic even though you have never worked before.

Working for startups

New companies, brands, and magazines always need a hand and very often the list of their requirements is not as long as that of a prestigious company. Unlike the big names of the industry, they don't have an endless list of people to choose from. Emerging brands, small companies, or startups want more than anything else to understand if you really care about the brand and if you want to contribute to growth. Therefore, the opportunities to get a job are much higher. Working for emerging brands or startups should be considered not only when you have little experience but also in any situation where it seems difficult to get a job working for the big names of the industry. If your goal is to work for large companies, you can always move to one later after gaining that little bit of experience you need at the startup. I have worked with some girls who contacted me online and I didn't focus on their CV because they had just graduated and some not even that. I always chose people who showed they knew Glam Observer and appreciated my mission by wanting to contribute to the project. It's easy to find interesting new brands and companies on Instagram to work with. You don't have to wait for them to post a job opening to reach out to them. The girls I worked with at Glam Observer have always contacted me on their own and I appreciated it even more. I admire the spirit of initiative and I consider that they contacted me not because they saw yet another open position to apply for, but because they are interested in the brand. When you work with these up-and-coming companies it's also easy to find opportunities remotely, so it's perfect to work from anywhere. You could propose to help with social media, to write content for their website or emails, for customer care, to take care of public relations, to be the founder's online assistant and organize their agenda, emails, etc. New companies are much more flexible in terms of requirements and ways of working, so they definitely need to be taken into consideration.

Social Media Manager

Helping a brand, a store in your city, or someone with social media is one of the most popular opportunities for those starting out in their careers. While in most careers companies are looking for someone with years of experience, when it comes to social media, youth has an advantage. Prepare a PDF with a weekly plan of what you would publish if you were to take care of that company's Instagram profile and send it to them. If you demonstrate that you can manage their social networks through this proposal, your CV will ultimately be irrelevant to them.

Showroom

Often showrooms are looking for some help, even for a short period of time, 1-2 weeks during a sales campaign. Even if your role will only be to welcome people, show the collection, bring coffee, or change flowers, it is still an experience that you can add to your resume. Furthermore, once you are in the showroom you will be in contact with various figures of the fashion sector: journalists and buyers that you could pass your CV to or collect their email address for future opportunities.

Remember that, thanks to the internet today, you can create your own experience by starting anything yourself: a blog where you publish your fashion articles, an online store where you sell t-shirts or jewelry created by you, an Instagram account where you post photos of your friends that you have styled and photographed. You can also design a collection and publish your portfolio online.

In fact, you can show your skills even without having a real experience at a company and get a job simply by showing your talent even when you do not have the requirements listed.

In addition to work experiences, you can also leverage your school years to bring out your skills. Did you write a fashion dissertation or did you work on a fashion-related project during your studies? For example, when I was studying for my master's I worked on projects for Versace and Estée Lauder and I included them both in the description of the master's program on my resume when I was looking for my first internship. If your university has allowed you to do an internship even for a couple of days at a company, add this experience separately to your studies and list it as if it were an experience in itself. You could also add a list of lessons you think are related to the position: digital marketing, writing, competitor analysis, market analysis, Excel, graphic design Photoshop, mood board creation, communication, styling.

Online courses are not great only to gain knowledge and expertise but also to enrich your resume.

20

COVER LETTER
AND
FASHION PORTFOLIO

COVER LETTER

Even more important than your resume is your cover letter. Especially when you are still starting out and your CV will likely be short and composed mainly of your studies, the cover letter will really make a difference in the application.

While the resume is schematic and cold, just a list of skills and experiences, the cover letter should show your emotions, passions, and motivations that make you the ideal candidate for that job.

In the cover letter, the list of skills you added to your CV comes to life with concrete examples and explains why they should hire you.

The cover letter is not just a recap of your resume so don't repeat the name of the school you went to, but explain how that school or a job taught you things that make you the best candidate for that company. You will have to express why you want to work there, what you like about that company and that position, and the values you share.

The cover letter must be absolutely personalized. While for CVs you can rearrange the order of the descriptions of the activities and skills but leave the same structure, for the cover letter you will have to start over every time you apply for a new job. If you've written a cover letter that you can use for more than one job, then it's not effective enough. Every job and every company requires different things and therefore in order to specify how your skills intersect with those required, it is impossible to use the same cover letter for multiple jobs.

When you are at the beginning of your career, all of your passion for the fashion industry must shine through in your cover letter and you must make the company understand your desire to work there, to learn quickly, to get involved, and to be willing to always give 100% for the brand you admire. If you have not studied fashion or want to switch to fashion after an experience in another industry, you will have to explain in the cover letter why you want to work in fashion now.

In addition to personalization, another factor that makes the cover letter effective is to address it to the right person.

It is important to find the email contact of the recruiter,

manager, editor, stylist and send the letter to the correct person, making sure that you spell the name correctly.

FASHION PORTFOLIO

If you want to become a designer, stylist, art director, photographer, journalist, or publicist you need a portfolio to send along with your resume and cover letter.

Many people tend to think that a portfolio is something reserved only for those who have attended a fashion school, but in reality, anyone can and should have it.

The portfolio is a collection of your works. Imagine a mini book consisting of photos, texts, and videos(if it's digital) which provide a multidimensional look at your skills. I said many times now in this book that showing your skills is the best way to get a job. The portfolio is generally used above all for the more creative careers that I mentioned above because they are the ones where you need to show creativity and your own unique style. As always, if you can customize the portfolio and add even just a page dedicated to that brand, obviously your chances of success will increase. Are you contacting an accessory or clothing brand? Do you want to write for *Teen Vogue* or *WWD*? Do you want to work with celebrities or style editorial campaigns? Based on where you are applying, you should show the skills that best suit that company in your portfolio.

For a fashion designer, the portfolio will be a collection of sketches, mood boards, inspirational images, photos taken of their own pieces or fabric samples, CAD drawings ... In short, everything that is useful to understand the whole process, from research and development to the final product. There is no need to have a thirty-page portfolio. Select the best jobs that you think may be of the most interest to that company. If you've been designing both shoes and clothing and now want to apply for a shoe brand, show more of your shoe-related work. If you are at the beginning of your career you can add your personal project in your portfolio to prove your skills and talent.

For an aspiring fashion journalist, the portfolio will be a collection of clips: articles published in magazines, your blog, or even still living on your desktop. A writing portfolio is even more important than your CV to get a job as a fashion writer, because in the end, an editor wants to know your writing style. A good article is a good article, it doesn't matter what you studied, if you don't have experience, or if these articles are just living on your blog, your Google Drive folder or have been published on Vogue. Do you remember the scene in which the friend advised Rebecca in *Confessions of a Shopaholic* to write an article to demonstrate how she was talented and a great writer and that she deserved a job at a fashion magazine? Well, maybe avoid the mistake of replacing the two letters, but the point is that it really works to show directly what you are capable of rather than hoping that the recruiter will get everything from your CV. The purpose of a portfolio is exactly that. Let your work do the talking for you.

For a stylist, the portfolio will include a series of photos of looks for which she has curated the styling: campaigns for magazines, editorials for brands, people and celebrities she has dressed for red carpets and events.

For those who want to work in PR this could be photos of organized events or examples of written press releases.

For a photographer, the portfolio will be a collection of shots.

Choose your preferred program to collect your works and build your portfolio: PowerPoint, Photoshop, InDesign or other presentation or graphic design software. Print the portfolio only when you need to meet someone in person and to go to an interview.

At all other times, when you apply online and via email, send your portfolio in PDF format or the link to your website.

Add the link to your portfolio everywhere: Instagram, LinkedIn, in the signature of your emails.

When you decide to get serious with your career you need to create a professional email that you will use for all communication and add to your resume, Instagram bio, and LinkedIn. Do not use a school email or one you created years ago such as ilovechanel@gmail.com. Use your name and surname. You might think it is an irrelevant detail but I assure you that it immediately gives you a professional air that people notice.

21

NAILING
YOUR FASHION JOB
INTERVIEW

"Hello?"

"Hello _____..., your profile is interesting, we would like to ask you a few questions and invite you for an interview."

Receiving an invitation to a job interview is always an exciting two-phase moment: first of all you are excited because your favorite company has chosen you and wants to meet, so you are one step closer to your job. However, immediately afterwards, anxiety begins about how to behave and what to say during the 30-60 minutes face-to-face with the recruiter and in most cases, even your future boss, to convince them that you are the ideal person for that job.

Don't panic. The adrenaline and nervousness are normal, but try to stay focused or too much anxiety could become a problem.

The best way to arrive confidently to a job interview is obviously to be prepared.

It's like going to a college exam. Depending on your level of preparation you will feel more or less confident, right?

Well, while exams can sometimes be retaken if you fail, with job interviews there are no second chances. This is not to make you more anxious but to encourage you to arrive with all of the information possible. Fortunately, the information you need to remember before an interview is much less than that of an exam, as you are about to see. Less information but that you need to remember well.

The first thing to do is research the company. NEVER go to an interview without having done research on the company.

Ideally, if you applied for that company you should have already done your research to personalize your application and adapt it to that position. But to be on the safe side let's start from scratch.

Go to Google, type in the company name and read as much content as you can about the brand with which you will have the interview.

Starting with the official website, first visit the About and Company Value/Mission pages and take note of the fundamental data. *Write this information in a notebook so you can quickly review it before the interview.*

Check the year the company was founded, and who the CEO and creative director are. Review collections or magazine covers and note which one is your favorite and why. See if the brand promotes social initiatives such as supporting women or sustainability. For example, if you are applying at Dior you should mention the mentoring women@dior program.

After you read everything on the brand website, go to Google again and this time read all the latest articles about the company, type in the name of your future boss, read if he or she has released any interviews and use LinkedIn to find out more about your future team.

Also check out the brand's social profiles and subscribe to the newsletter to keep an eye on marketing campaigns.

After that, print or open the job description and read it carefully.

My first internship was as an E-commerce Account for Alexander McQueen. Obviously the main activity was the management of the online store but also of the brand's newsletters.

Before the interview I visited the site and clicked on everything clickable! The various pages, all the products; I also tried to add a product to the cart to simulate a purchase (I didn't complete it because AMQ was out of my budget, but if it's a cheap product you can also think about finalizing the purchase to see the whole experience including the delivery). If I got the job I had to support managing the e-commerce so I identified myself with the role and started browsing the site. I wanted to learn how the site worked, what the various pages were, how the products were divided (new arrivals, shoes, bags, accessories, clothes ...) and I also thought of solutions for how I would eventually modify the site. The site was fully functional, but when I signed up for the newsletter and I did the same by clicking on all the links, I realized that a link was not working, it was not clickable. I wrote it down and impressed the manager during the interview by reporting this information.

Reading the job description thoroughly before an interview is essential in helping you understand what else you might be researching.

Reviewing Excel and all the programs mentioned in the job offer is also a valuable way to feel and be more prepared.
There are multiple interview steps for the same position, even if it is an internship! Generally the first step is more generic and cognitive. You are asked to tell them about yourself, what you studied, your previous experiences, why you applied, why you care about that brand, why they should hire you.

The second and third can also be cognitive but include other people: a second recruiter or someone from the team; or it can be a test. At my second interview, I took an Excel test. They put me in front of a laptop with an open Excel table and sales data. I had to calculate the sell through and other sales (knowing pivot tables and basic functions like VLOOKUP can be lifesaving at these stages!)

Then they asked me to order products as if I were going to create the new arrivals page on the alexandermcqueen.com site. During this phase my advice is to think aloud, because even if you don't get to the final result but your logic works, it's still fine. Especially for an internship, they know you're there to learn and they want to see your way of thinking.

At this point, after having
1. studied the brand
2. read the job description
3. reviewed programs such as Photoshop, Excel, and other relevant programs

it's time to prepare your elevator speech.

Your elevator speech is how you introduce yourself to the brand on the first icebreaker question: tell us a little about yourself. Beginning the conversation is always the hardest part of the job interview, but since most of them will start with this question it is best to practice the answer so the interview starts off well. First impressions count!

Practice your elevator speech at home. It is called an elevator speech because in the time it takes you in an elevator ride to go to the upper floors you should be able to explain who you are to whoever is with you in the elevator.

See the job interview as an opportunity for discussion and exchanging information, not just a moment for the company to evaluate you.

You too have to see if the company and that position is right for you. Always prepare a couple of questions to ask at the end of the interview. You could perhaps ask how a typical working day goes to understand from the list of activities listed in the job description which are the main ones and the ones that will take you the most time or who you'll be working with. If the interview makes you anxious, think that whoever is in front of you is also at a critical moment in their work. Finding the right person to hire is never an easy job. Hiring the wrong person makes a company lose an average of $50,000 per year. So the recruiter will also be under pressure to do their job well during the job interview and, if they don't make you feel at ease, it might probably be that they feel uncomfortable too because they feel the pressure of hiring the right person.

Your goal during the interview should in fact be to "reassure" the recruiter that you are the person who is committed, faithful, who learns quickly, works hard, and cares about the company and will do your best to contribute to its growth.

Remember to always be concrete every time you explain your competence. Without using vague language, simply say: I'm good at doing X, Y, and Z.

Give practical examples that prove your skills, even refer to relevant situations from your university if you are at the beginning of your career:

"I'm good at public speaking because during university I had the opportunity to give five presentations a year in front of the class and the professors."

"I'm a highly organized person; in one weekend I organized the entire school library by genres."

"I took three exams in math and economics so I know the basic functions of Excel and I'm ready to learn everything else even by myself to be the best at my job."

Google is your best friend today; don't be afraid to say that you will be able to find a solution, because online you can find the answer to everything: from how to use Photoshop to what "sell in or sell out" are. All you need is the desire to learn and you can learn anything. Show your initiative and willingness to learn and strive to be their best resource. Study the job description well and identify what the key things are for that job. Then think about how you can explain to the company that you have those skills by referring to concrete experiences. Prepare in advance a list of your skills that you think are needed for that job and how you will be able to apply them to the company. In this way you are answering their question on why they should hire you over other candidates.

In addition to making references to past episodes and experiences, bring your portfolio to show your skills during the job interview. If you are interviewing with a fashion magazine bring articles that you've written, if it's a social media job, bring the PDF with an outline of content that you would post on their

Instagram account for a week. If it's a fashion design job, bring your design portfolio whether you've created it with the support of a fashion school or by yourself working on personal projects.

The Online Interview

If you have applied for a company that is in a different country, you can request or be requested to do a first interview online on Skype or Zoom. The way to prepare for an online interview is identical. Just because it's over the phone or Skype doesn't mean it's less important. Especially because of the global pandemic, many companies have hired directly from online interviews! So it might also be your only selection step. If you've never used Skype or Zoom, do a test by calling your friend first to familiarize yourself with the platform and avoid hitches on the day of the interview.

Check your username and make sure it's professional like you did with your email address. You have to share your username with the company so I'm sure you want it to be professional and not the username you chose to create your first account years ago: name.ilovemydog.
If this is the case, it is better to create a new one.
If you do not have a Skype or Zoom account, create one, but never tell the company that you don't have one and would prefer to make a call.
Choose a room where you won't be disturbed during the

interview and make sure everything is in order; even better if you can use a simple white wall as a background. Set aside at least an hour of time, silence your phone, and make sure you have a good connection that allows you to have a smooth conversation without interruption. Before the interview, you can do a test with a friend or just turn on the webcam to understand your position: show yourself from the chest up. You may choose to use headphones for better sound.

In general, online job interviews are video calls, not just audio, so no pajamas even if you will be at home. Dress and do your makeup as if you were going to an in-person interview. Also, your attitude during the call should be professional. Sit in a comfortable chair and avoid moving too much. This will be your first impression to the company so try to be spontaneous but professional.

Make sure you have your resume in front of you (possibly without making it appear in the camera) because, they will use that to start and ask questions during the job interview. You can also have your notes on hand with company data, names of the CEO, creative director, various stylists, and a list of the company's most important events, as well as the questions you would like to ask them.

What to do after an interview

Once the interview is over, whether it's online or in person, your work does not end there. Immediately after the interview, send an email to all the people you interviewed with. Generally you should have the email address of at least one person who invited you to the job interview and sent the details of the meeting. If you don't have it, or if you want the address of someone else who was present at the interview as well, don't be afraid to ask for their contact information at the end of the job interview.

In the email, thank them for their time and the opportunity by saying that it was a pleasure to meet them and that you look forward to hearing back from them.

If during the interview you forgot to say something important or you want to rephrase a sentence that came out wrong, this is the time to include those details you may have left out. Apologize for being nervous during the interview and explain what you wanted to say.

Remember that following up is essential here too. If during the interview they told you that they are in the selection process and that they will let you know within two weeks, wait two weeks and if you have not received any news, send an email and ask if they have had time to think about your profile and if they need more information.

What to wear at a job interview.

Many people ask me what to wear to an interview. What you wear represents who you are, so be professional but still yourself. If you've been following Glam Observer for a while, you know that the pink jacket (the one I also put on the cover) is my brand. It's a photo I took and then it was used by Forbes when they put me on the Under 30 list, I also wore it to my second fashion panel in Milan and I generally think it represents me. If I had to do an interview I think I'd put that on. If you don't want to go wrong, a black jacket and a t-shirt or blouse are always the right choice. It's all in your personality and also depends on the company; if the company is more corporate you may want to dress up. If it's a startup, it's usually acceptable to dress casually. Consider what type of company it is and your personality and dress accordingly.

So let's recap what to do:

• study the brand
• read the job description carefully to identify the keywords
• review programs such as Photoshop, Excel, CAD...
• practice your elevator speech
• wear something professional but that represents you and makes you feel confident and comfortable
• if you have an online interview, prepare as if it were in person
• Send a thank you email at the end of any interview step

• Follow up on time if you have no news from the company

Now that we've seen what to do, let's find out what NOT to do at a job interview.

• Obviously, never be late for a job interview. Better to calculate in advance with Google Maps how long it will take you to arrive and leave thirty minutes in advance to avoid any potential traffic or hitch that might make you late. Don't arrive too early either; 10-15 minutes earlier is enough. If you have been given an appointment, respect it.

• Being nervous is normal, but do not reveal yourself to be too nervous during your job interview with a fashion company. Be confident about your abilities, but be careful that this doesn't appear as smug. A great way to look confident is to always look the person you are talking to in the eye rather than looking down or looking around. Being able to contain anxiety also helps the recruiter to understand how you react in stressful situations when you are under pressure, which often happens in fashion. When we are nervous we tend to make some movements that we might not notice at the moment, such as drumming one leg, fidgeting in the chair, rubbing hands. Body language says a lot about your personality and recruiters notice what you do in addition to what you say, so be careful to check these nervous movements and don't forget to smile! Everyone wants to work with other people who are kind and pleasant to be around, so smile.

- Don't ask about the salary in the first step of a job interview. This will be a discussion during the last round of interviews or when they offer you the job.

- Despite having warned friends and family not to call you during that time frame of your interview, always set the phone to silent or turn it off to avoid embarrassing interruptions from a random call or any notification sounds.

- Even if your former boss was the worst, the recruiter doesn't know the truth. They only hear your version, so avoid any negative comments about your old job and team. Bad-mouthing a previous employer only makes the person who is interviewing you worry about what you might say about them or that maybe you don't work well in a team because you quarreled with all your colleagues. Instead, be neutral and mention what you have learned and above all what you would like to learn now.

PART IV
Master Your Fashion Boss Skills

22

CONFIDENCE IS A SKILL
(+ All the Others You Need

"I don't have the skills to work in fashion."

I have heard this statement as many times as the ones we have already discussed—I didn't study fashion, I have no experience—but what are the skills that you *really* need to work in fashion?

We have reached the last part of this book, so by now we should know that working in fashion means everything and nothing. Since we now know that there are so many different careers in fashion, we can assume that the skills required cannot be the same for all jobs in this industry. There are obviously soft skills that are applicable to every role just as there are those that characterize every single career.

The technical skills of a designer will not be the same as the skills needed for working in PR. In fact, not everyone who works in fashion knows how to design clothes or sew, just as the team of designers doesn't need to be as extroverted as those who work in PR, whose job it is to communicate all day, every day.

Before talking about various skills, I would like to address another fundamental point:
competence is not the same as talent.
While talent is a gift that you are born with and that with practice you can perfect and refine a technique (such as singing, dancing, or drawing for example), skills can be acquired. Awesome news, right? It means that you can no longer say that you don't have the right skills because every skill can be learned and the more you practice the more you can become an expert at something.

The main concept, that I hope you have taken from this book, is that you need to act and not sit idle to get what you want. From the moment you realize you need something for your career, you need to go and get it.
There is a positive side to the statement: "I don't have the skills for this job." It means you've identified them which is already a great thing. Identifying the skills needed for a job seems so difficult for so many people, but it's actually easier than you think. The company simply makes a list of requirements when posting a job offer and those are the skills you should have. You then evaluate that list and see what you can tick off that you

already have and what you need to acquire in order to apply.

Before assuming that you lack one or more of the skills required for a job, I would like to tell you that skills are not acquired only with work experience. I'm saying this especially if you are at the beginning of your career and you might think you don't have any skills to add to your resume. You certainly already have gained skills over the years from personal or school experiences that you might have overlooked so far.

Have you already worked on group projects during university? Teamwork ✓

Do you have an agenda with you? Do you always respect appointments? Do you like planning? Organization ✓

Are you the social person in a group and do you enjoy talking to people? Communication ✓

Skills can be grouped mainly into two categories: technical skills and the so-called soft skills. Before listing them, I want to talk about what I think is the most useful skill in every career and at every stage of a professional path: from your first internship to when you become the CEO, Senior Manager, or Editor in Chief:

Self-Confidence.

This is the only skill you really need in your career.

Lack of self-confidence is the most common problem that I find in any email or message you send.

I can't work in fashion because I didn't studied fashion.
I don't have the right skills.
I don't have enough experience.
I'm not good enough.
The best companies will never consider me.
I can't find a job.

At the base of all these false assumptions lies a lack of self-confidence.

Let me tell you something that might change your opinion on confidence.
<u>No one is born confident. Confidence is not a talent, it is a skill.</u>
<u>And we have just said that any skill can be acquired and that the</u>
<u>more you practice, the better you become at it.</u>
Confidence is something you acquire over time. If you live in a family that has always encouraged you, you are lucky because you were exposed to self-confidence from an early age. But if you still feel you are lacking this skill, you can develop it by practicing every single day.
There are obviously those who are more inclined toward it and manage to develop it faster or better, but confidence is not something just for extroverts; even if you are shy you can build the dose of confidence you need.

Most of the time, a lack of self-confidence is linked to the fear of failure.

What happens if, as you believe, you fail? I want you to think about the worst-case scenario.

Seriously.

What's the worst that can happen if you apply for a job at Gucci?

Or if you send an email to a stylist to ask if they need an assistant?

That they are going to ignore your application or say they are looking for someone with different skills?

What's the worst that can happen if you start your own fashion brand?

That it doesn't take off? That no buyer wants to stock it? That you will have to quit and find another job?

What's the worst that can happen if you send your articles to the editor to get published in that fashion magazine?

That they don't read them? That they say it's not good or that they're not interested? That they don't get back to you at all?

And tell me, was it really that scary? Can an email really scare you that much? Because that's what it is.

Nowadays, trying your luck is even easier and faster. How many people could you reach out to via email in a single day? Can you imagine if you had to go in front of someone to ask for a job? In that case, you'd need even more courage. But today the first approach (which is also the most difficult) in 97% of cases happens online via email. You're "safe" behind your laptop or smartphone and it's definitely not as awkward as in person. Even if you receive a negative response, it's just an email. It might be sad perhaps at first because you wanted that opportunity, but has your life changed?

Has that email hit you physically so that you can't move tomorrow, or that can't you apply for another job today? Have you taken a step back from where you were by sending that application or that email or launching your brand?

NO, NO, and NO.

Going for it and failing is the equivalent of not doing it at all out of fear.

But what if someone tells you *YES*?

Instead of focusing on what would happen if you fail, why don't you start asking yourself today:

How would my life change if it happens?

If I apply for that job and I get it, I will finally start working for my dream brand! Amazing!
If I email that editor, my name could be in that fashion magazine! Hell yes!
If I launch my brand, Net-a-Porter could sell it on their site, I could open

my own store in more cities and sell online all over the world, and celebrities would wear my clothes!

Do you see how many incredible opportunities you could have, simply by deciding to have the courage to do it?

The worst options, the "failures," the negative answers, don't have an impact on your life. You may be sad the first few days, but your life is not going backwards, you get stronger and each *no* hurts less and less than the previous ones.

While at the first YES you receive, your life finally changes, taking exactly the direction you desire.

And tell me, do you really prefer to stay like this and not get what you want because you are too intimidated to send an email? I'm sure you don't. Not at this point in the book. I'm sure you have big plans for yourself.

The things that would happen if you are successful are a thousand times better than the consequences if it doesn't go well.

The next time you're intimidated by something or someone and can't decide whether to take action or not, ask yourself these two questions: What's the worst that can happen if I fail? What if it works?

The more you practice confidence, the more you'll ask yourself only the second question, not doubting at all or considering the bad things. The more you practice confidence, the more you learn that a single YES wipes out all the NOs received and that failure is only a learning opportunity!

Failing is part of the process. It is inevitable. It is the first step towards success. Everyone fails. You just have to accept it and move on. Your strategies and emails may fail, but you are not the failure.

Failure is an opportunity to learn.

What can you learn today so you can do better tomorrow?

Did your job application fail? Well, you may need to edit your CV, write your cover letter again, and customize it perfectly for that position. You might need to change your application strategies, or email recruiters directly to have a better chance of getting noticed and standing out.

Having self-confidence means believing that you can complete any task, regardless of the difficulty.

It means making mistakes and continuing to make them but learning from them and moving forward.

We are almost at the end of this book and since I have written it in order, this is one of the last chapters that I am writing. Today I sent an email to Imran Amed, yes, the founder of *The Business of Fashion*, asking him if he would like to write a blurb for my book, which is one of those quotes you see on book covers with others' opinions about the book. How it will end we will all see when this book is published (still today, two days later when I am editing what I wrote, I have not received an answer). But the point is, I didn't think about what might happen if he doesn't get back to me or what he might have thought of me reading that email. I've just focused on how awesome it would be if he did respond. Yes, it took me thirty minutes to write that email and proofread it (this is normal), but then I hit send.

In 2011, Bronnie Ware published a book about her time as a nurse and documented the five biggest regrets of people on their deathbeds. The number one regret was: I would like to have had the courage to live a truer life for myself and not worry about what others expect from me.

Now I don't want to be melodramatic, but the reality is you have one life. And I want you to experience it to the fullest. Don't let fear of failure or the judgment of others stop you.

"What will they think of me?"

Let me tell you something else. People will always talk about you. Even when you think you just did the best thing in the world, people will always have to comment.

It's a bit like weddings. Couples organize their dream wedding for months and for them that's the perfect way to celebrate it, but you may have a different opinion. As much as everyone plans their ideal wedding, there will always be someone who will have something negative to say.

The same is true for each of us. Whatever you do, you will be judged. So you might as well do what you want and just listen to yourself.

Obviously this doesn't mean disrespecting someone or being rude without worrying about someone's feelings. I'm referring to all those moments when you wanted to do something— launch your own project, email someone, introduce yourself to a person—and you stopped, because you worried about their opinion.

Remind yourself that you will never be criticized by someone who is doing more than you, but by someone who is doing less.

Just by getting rid of the fear of failure by accepting it and considering it part of the process, and not caring about the opinions of everyone, you will significantly increase your confidence.

Other ways to develop this competence are:

1. Act confident even when you are not yet 100% convinced (Fake it until you make it!)

2. Share your ideas, opinions, projects ... talk about them with conviction and confidence with whoever you are talking to. To convince others you must first be convinced yourself.

3. Obviously, in order to speak with conviction, you have to make sure that you are not saying things that are not true or that you have not been able to verify. Listen more and talk when needed, not just for the sake of saying something. I speak

little and listen a lot and tend to express an opinion only when I know I can contribute or if I'm sure of what I'm saying. If I am not an expert on the subject or have never heard of it, I prefer to do some research first and just listen in the meantime.

4. Maintain eye contact with everyone, including the CEO.

5. Wearing your favorite blazer might help in some situations.

6. Learn. When I told you in Part II to introduce learning into your daily activities, I anticipated that, among other things, it's also useful for confidence-building. We are all more confident when we know the topic we will talk about, how things work, and how to behave. Like the example of taking an exam that we talked about in the job interview chapter, you feel more confident if you studied because you know what to answer. In this book I have tried to include as much information as possible so that you know what to expect and practice what to do.

And you should also have started thinking with the new I-can-figure-everything-out mindset. Are you afraid that during the job interview for a buyer or merchandising role they'll ask you to do an Excel exercise, but you don't know how to use it? Well, go online and learn it before the interview. Do you want to work in Paris but French in your weakness? Take French lessons online today. Are you afraid that they will ask you some questions about the brand during the job interview and you don't know how to answer? Study the brand.

Acquire any skill that causes you insecurity!
Being insecure is not a permanent condition.

Having self-confidence means believing that you can learn and face everything. Which is the reason why I believe this is the most important skill for your career, and why I wanted to deepen it more than any other.

In this book I couldn't cover everything, or it would have been too long, and my courses would not exist, but I wanted to give you the key tips so that you can figure out the rest.

Becoming confident is not something that's only in your best interest, but people enjoy being surrounded by confident people, especially companies looking for job candidates.

Master confidence and you'll get any other requirements.

OTHER SKILLS YOU SHOULD PRACTICE FOR YOUR CAREER IN FASHION.

1. Excel

For some careers as buyers, merchandisers, those who work in marketing ... having a good knowledge of Excel is mandatory, but in general, every person who works in fashion will have to deal with Excel (yes, even designers) to organize data and contacts, keep track of sales, and analyze performances. Some less and some more, but every company requires at least a basic understanding of Excel, so learn the basics. Knowing the rest of the Office suite, especially PowerPoint and Word, is obviously important as well.

2. Photoshop, InDesign, Illustrator, CAD

Knowing these programs is essential for some careers but not for all. For those who want to deal with graphics and design, advertising, art direction and social media ... the more your job involves creating graphics, the more you need to master these tools. Before taking an advanced Photoshop course, read a couple of job descriptions of your ideal role and see if that's a required skill and if it's the main part of the job or just good to know. Even if it's not required, having a knowledge of something outside of your responsibilities is always useful in case you can save a situation in your office.

3. Passion

This soft skill is essential for a career in fashion, whatever department you want to get into. Passion is the key ingredient of success, the engine that will push you to keep going even on hard days, and that will make even the boring tasks, like bringing coffee or making photocopies, enjoyable simply because you love what you do. Especially during your internship, companies want to hire people who are enthusiastic, and have energy and passion for the job and the company. Companies know that those who are driven by passion can learn anything else on the job.

4. Organizational skills

Interns/assistants who work at a fashion magazine, assist stylists, or work in PR, spend most of their time organizing closets, keeping track of samples that arrive for photo shoots, unpacking and packing clothes, sending them back to brands, keeping the archive in order, organizing contact databases ... Organization is the basis of every job well-executed. An organized person knows what is necessary for a job and the tasks to reach the end goal, and delivers it on time without forgetting pieces on the way. Organizational skills show responsibility and will guarantee you trust from your boss and the whole team.

5. Social Media

If you want to work with social media it is obvious that you must have a knowledge of all the platforms: Instagram, Facebook, Twitter, Pinterest, TikTok ... knowing them does not mean only for personal use. Read articles to stay informed about updates, read reports on influencer marketing, and how companies use social media strategies in their campaigns, what are the KPIs (Key Performance Indicators) that companies consider when analyzing the performance of campaigns, and how the advertising works on these platforms.

6. Wordpress and SEO

If you want to write for an online magazine you should know the basics of Wordpress and a little SEO. The company may ask you to upload your articles directly to the platform and write them respecting the SEO rules. You can learn everything for free on Google.

7. Fashion Design

Together with the soft skills mentioned here, those who want to work as fashion designers need to master these technical skills: sketching, pattern making and draping, illustration, CAD design, knowledge of the fabrics and which one to choose among all the samples (even during a job interview), and hand/machine sewing skills.

8. Excellent written and verbal communication skills

It goes without saying that communication skills are required in every role, but are especially crucial in PR, Marketing, and Social Media, where your job is to communicate: convey the brand message through a social post, a YouTube video, an advertising campaign or an event, communicate to the right audience in a creative and persuasive way, build and maintain relationships with the press ... Having excellent verbal and written communication skills is absolutely necessary for anyone's job. Bad communication in PR means damaging the brand image, losing sales and customers, and for anyone else in the company, it implies misunderstandings that lead to delays or errors. Therefore it is one of those soft skills that everyone should work on.

9. Languages

Fashion is an international industry and you'll get in touch with people from many cultures and countries. Especially in big companies that have offices around the world, you might find yourself talking with a buyer in New York, a designer in Milan, and a PR firm in London in the same day. That's why companies usually require employees who speak more than one language: English, French, and Italian are the most popular for any corporate job. If you want to work in China or deal with the Chinese market within your company, this is another language you should study.

10. History of fashion

Developing a knowledge of fashion history is typically more of a skill that you *want* to learn rather than *have* to learn. If you are passionate about this industry you'll want to learn anything and everything: the designers who made history, which designers are at which brands, how the various cultural movements were born, and all the rest. Read books, take online courses, watch videos on YouTube, and fashion documentaries (you can find many on Netflix and Amazon Prime). Here are some worth checking out:

The September Issue	*Diana Vreeland: The Eye Has to Travel*
Dior And I	*Lagerfeld Confidential*
Westwood: Punk. Icon. Activist	*McQueen*
Martin Margiela: In His Own Words	*Franca: Chaos and Creation*
Valentino: The Last Emperor	*Very Ralph*
The Boy Who Made Shoes For Lizards	*The Supermodels*

11. Knowledge of the industry

Fashion is not just about creativity, it's a business. The ideal would be that you are both left-and right-brained. Left-brained people are thought to be more analytical and those who are right-brained are considered to be more creative or artistic ... I believe that if you want to succeed in fashion you should have a balance.

We said that with Google today you have no more excuses not to stay updated every day on what happens in the fashion world and you can learn from books, podcasts, and videos. It is important to know who the key players are in the market, what the trends are (not only in style, but also current issues such as sustainability or inclusiveness), what are the growing markets, and how competitors are moving. You don't want to arrive on your first day at the office and not be able to plug into a conversation because you haven't heard the latest news of the day about an LVMH or Kering acquisition of another brand, or the appointment of a new creative director.

Nowadays, the more transversal and flexible you are with your skills, the better. Especially when you are at the beginning of your career; during your internship you may be asked to do many different kinds of tasks. So having a little knowledge of everything never hurts. Be curious and never stop learning everything about fashion, but not just fashion.

23

CAREERS IN THE
FASHION INDUSTRY

As we all know, the fashion industry is made up of different careers. I wanted to include in this book a quick introduction to some of the careers in fashion but there are still many more roles in addition to these. As I said before, fashion is not just about creativity but it's also a business, so all the typical departments exist inside a fashion company: finance, legal, marketing, and of course, design. I have included careers from different departments, not just the most creative ones, and listed some of their activities to give you an idea of these careers, but they are not limited to these. The responsibilities could be different according to the company and country. So I recommend reading a job description carefully before applying, to see what job activities are at a specific company.

In fashion you can work in-house at a brand, agency, online retailer (Net-a-Porter, MyTheresa, MatchesFashion, LuisaViaRoma), department stores (La Rinascente, Harrods, Saks Fifth Avenue, Macy's, Selfridges), or magazine, or you can work as a freelancer and work on a project basis, and not as an employeee of a company. The most common freelance roles are stylist, photographer, editor, consultant, writer, copywriter, social media manager, designer, and art director. As a freelancer, your responsibility is to find clients.

I also want to remind you again to not consider only big, established brands but also new designers, niche fashion magazines, and startups. Almost all the roles described below can be found either at a big brand or an emerging one.

FASHION MAGAZINE
EDITOR IN CHIEF

If you watched *The Devil Wears Prada* and dream about sitting at Miranda Priestley's desk (or Anna Wintour's), you should know the pathway to becoming an EIC requires lots of hard work and years of experience. Most Editor in Chiefs start out in entry-level positions usually as Interns, Junior Editors, Assistant Editors, or Editorial Assistants—and work their way up from there, to become Associate Editor, Senior Editor, Deputy Editor, and finally, Editor in Chief.

An Editor in Chief is the manager of a publication, whether it is digital, print, or both. They determine the scope, tone, and content of the publication while overseeing the content, writing, hiring of editors and photographers, and managing the budget.

FASHION EDITORS

The Fashion Editor has the ultimate responsibility for everything that gets published. Fashion Editors take care of the pitching, reporting, writing, editing, and publishing of all articles. They also decide on the styling for shoots and attend fashion shows and events.

ADVERTISING MANAGER

If you want to work at a fashion magazine but you are more interested in the business side of it, you should consider the advertising department. Advertising is a magazine's biggest source of income. The advertising team is responsible for selling pages of the magazine to advertisers; negotiating rates; managing relationships with clients; and liaising with the editorial team to create advertorial articles.

FASHION INTERN

If you want to become a Fashion Editor at a fashion magazine you will start your career as a Fashion Intern or Fashion Assistant and your activities will include: managing the fashion closet; organizing returns; sending out emails; cleaning and filing; transcribing and research tasks; helping to pull clothes for shoots; assisting the stylist on photo shoots; keeping note of the credits needed to include in the magazine for each item; and even writing short stories.

DESIGN

CREATIVE DIRECTOR

Today this role no longer begins and ends with designing collections, in fact the Creative Director is helped by an entire team of designers.

A Creative Director is responsible for the overall creative aesthetic of a brand, developing and executing an all-encompassing vision; advertising campaigns; store design; social media strategy and brand collaborations; the format of the catwalk presentations; and the lifestyle that the brand is selling, also considering management's input. A Creative Director needs to also understand the marketing and merchandising strategies. Hence the term, Creative Director, as opposed to "designer."

FASHION DESIGNER

There is an entire team of designers inside a fashion brand (especially the biggest names) who work on the collections. It's not just about the Creative Director. Designers are overseen by the Design Director, leaving to the Creative Director the time and ability to oversee the big picture for the brand.

Responsibilities of Designers include development of the collections across all categories; design research; preparation of visual tools; creating mood and color boards; coordinating with the product team to ensure alignment with collection launches; fabric allocation; styling and coordinating collection looks; and other pre-show preparations.

FASHION DESIGN INTERN

If you want to become a Designer, you'll need to start as an intern like in any other career. Design Interns are usually responsible for assisting in creating and maintaining mood and style development boards; researching trends and colors; photographing new development samples or mock-ups; assisting with hand sewing; helping the team to prepare for meetings with vendors and buyers; assisting in ordering, receiving, and keeping records of development fabrics; sourcing fabrics; technical flat sketching or Photoshop CADs; costing out all of the components needed for a garment's production; developing line sheets and supportive materials; assisting during sketch presentations, fittings, style-outs, or fabric development meetings.

ART DIRECTOR

Art Directors work both at fashion magazines and brands but the activities are different.

An Art Director of a fashion magazine is in charge of the overall visual style, layout, and graphic design of the publication. A typical day for an Art Director involves visual meetings with the editors and the fashion department and managing a team of in-house and freelance photographers, stylists, models, and hair/makeup artists on photo shoots and video shoots. This role requires managerial skills to work with graphic designers, copywriters, journalists, influencers, advertising professionals, and media buyers, within certain budgets and deadlines. And also design skills, an Art Director knows how to use InDesign, Photoshop, Illustrator Premiere Pro, or Final Cut and After Effects.

The main role of the Art Director who works with a brand is to ensure that the company's vision and brand image is consistent, globally, across all platforms. The Art Director works with the Creative Director on developing the image strategy from concept to delivery for advertising, media, social, e-commerce, supporting collateral, packing, and trims. Like at a fashion publication, at a fashion brand the Art Director also collaborates with the styling teams on photo sets, as well as pre- and post- production.

MARKETING, COMMUNICATION, AND MANAGEMENT

DIGITAL MARKETING MANAGER

The marketing department plans and executes the marketing strategies for the brand according to the direction of the Creative Director and Brand Director to establish key brand priorities and integrate them with key product/seasonal priorities and grow the brand and the business. The Digital Marketing Manager is responsible for all the online marketing activities of the website (SEO, SEM, paid social) affiliate marketing program, and email marketing campaign strategy. They also measure performances to make sure the digital presence is world-class.

CRM CUSTOMER RELATIONSHIP MANAGEMENT

CRM is that part of marketing that focuses on developing different marketing strategies according to the client's levels (from new clients to top spenders). Activities include maintaining and growing the client database through acquiring new clients and implementing retention strategies; analyzing data related to customer behavior; implementing personalized cross-channel campaigns (email, onsite, social, etc.); identifying rules to cluster dynamically the customer base; developing and iterating the digital customer journey and related analytics; analyzing and monitoring customer base KPIs; designing client gifting strategy; identifying areas for improvement and new business opportunities.

BRAND MANAGER

The Brand Manager takes care of creating, preserving, and shaping the identity of a brand. They work more on the business/management side of the brand, doing analysis on trends, customers, competitors, production, and inventory management, as well as developing new business plans and strategies.

FASHION BUYER

Clothes stocked in your favorite stores are not there just because the brand has produced that collection, but because the Buyer has decided which pieces of the collection to sell in that specific store. Fashion Buyers analyze previous data, feedback from store teams, trends, competitors, and customer behavior to predict what customers want and shape the season assortment to ensure maximum profit. They are also responsible for the stock: re-balancing, stock movement, monitoring daily, weekly, and monthly sales, deep-diving in category and sizing. They attend fashion weeks and presentations to discover the latest collections.

The role of the Buyer changes a lot from one company to another. Together with the Retail Buyer role that I've just explained, at a brand the Fashion Buyer could be responsible for sourcing fabrics and materials for the designers. Buyers work with merchandisers and in some companies the line between these two roles might be blurred so it's always better to read the job description carefully because a Buyer could do the job of a merchandiser and vice versa.

MERCHANDISER

When you look at the pieces making a new collection of a brand, is not just because the designers one morning woke up and decided to include dresses, shorts, pants or whatever they wanted. It's someone's job to say how many dresses, skirts, pants to include in a collection: the Collection Merchandiser who gives the collection guidelines to the designer based on analysis of the performance of the previous seasons, which pieces worked best, what are the new trends, colors, what the competitors are doing, what customers bought. The Collection Merchandiser elaborates the collection plan and identify new product opportunities that will drive revenue. The merchandiser builds the collection brief: functions, styles, materials and colors ,the pricing architecture in order to hit the company's target margins.

The Retail Merchandiser instead has a completely different role that in some companies is very similar to the one of the buyer. The Retail Merchandiser in fact works more with stores managing the product flow in order to deliver the merchandise in proper time, monitors and analyzes sales by product category/ boutique, implement the annual purchasing and merchandising budget, check inventories and sell-through data and follow-up operation such as daily/weekly re-assortment.

The Visual Merchandiser is the person who works in store and implement and maintain all visual directives and standards for interior merchandising, windows, and in store special events that follow the guidelines sent by the company.

ONLINE/WEBSITE MERCHANDISER

The job of the Site Merchandiser is to develop an ad hoc digital strategy to recreate the brand identity online, with the final aim of increasing sales, visits, and online brand awareness. The tasks include building an online calendar and making sure that all the messages are linked with the availability of products on the website; organizing the product pages (new arrivals, shoes, bags, dresses...); giving visual inputs to push products through every section of the website in order to make them easy to find and to create appealing and interesting navigation; suggesting trends and topics focused on the main markets to allow online localization and to make the best in terms of sales in every e-commerce area; indicate actions and tendencies of the main online competitors based on Benchmark and Research Analysis; elaborate plans and special activities to boost sales based on KPIs performances and analysis; work with the buying team to ensure that all the Open to Buy priorities are respected and aligned about seasonal collection and delivery drops; face with Commercial, User Experience, CRM and Web Marketing Team for website navigation, online commercial strategy and web performances.

SHOWROOM/WHOLESALE ASSISTANT

If you are interested in an entry-level role that deals with sales and marketing, you might consider joining a fashion brand as the Wholesale Intern/Assistant where you will deal with organizing selling campaigns and coordinating showroom appointments with clients; creating budget files; managing pre-market and post-market communications and general bookings with third parties (model casting, travel, accommodation, cleaning, security, etc.); assisting the sales team to input and amend sales orders; handle sample requests and returns from clients and wholesale partners for editorial photoshoots, e-commerce photoshoots, and general marketing content; general requests from clients such as product information files, campaign images, product images, branding content, official documentation, etc; assisting the sales team on reporting and data analysis; delivering show invites, buyer giftings.

INFLUENCER MARKETING MANAGER

The Influencer Marketing Manager is responsible for planning, executing, and delivering influencer activity. Tasks include cultivating and strengthening relationships with influencers; maintaining budget spending; coordinating and implementing influencer campaigns and events during product launches, fashion week, etc, and reporting.

SOCIAL MEDIA EDITOR

Social Media Editors work at fashion magazines, fashion brands, digital agencies, and online retailers. They manage the daily and weekly content calendars for all social channels; produce posts that drive traffic, engagement, and revenue; work with the design, picture, and video teams to create and choose relevant assets for all posts; review and report on performance of content on a daily, weekly, and monthly basis; and liaise between the content, marketing, e-commerce, fashion, press, and partnerships teams to ensure a joint approach to social media that meets business needs.

COPYWRITER

The Copywriter writes, develops, conveys, and maintains the brand voice in all print and digital assets, including ads, magazine, stories, store signage, newsletters, event invitations, websites, blog posts, e-commerce, and additional collateral materials.

PR MANAGER

The PR Manager is responsible for all the communication of the brand. What people, magazines, and others say and don't say about the brand is a responsibility of the PR Manager who develops and implements tailored communication strategies (print, digital, social); manages press features and distribution of press kits for the promotion of key PR initiatives (i.e. collections, events, store openings) in alignment with strategic objectives and KPIs; evaluate and facilitate interview and photo shoot requests in relation to the Creative Director;coordinate with various departments, including Merchandising, Global Communications, Marketing, and Media; define and manage the events calendar for Press, VIP, and Clients; plan and manage retail marketing activities, events, press days, and fashion shows; maintain existing and new media lists and databases; monitor all outlets for brand mentions; manage any negative press/crisis communication sensitively to optimize the company reputation.

PR INTERN

PR internships are the most popular in fashion and for many it's their first job in this industry, even those who end up working in a different department (editorial, merchandising, design...).You can intern in the PR department of a brand or in a PR agency that manages multiple brands.The responsibilities of a PR Intern mainly include organizing samples; supplying credits information to all magazines; preparing press clippings; packing and unpacking clothes to ship to editors and stylists for campaigns; assisting on event organization and support on event day (press days, fashion shows, product launches, influencers' events..).

STYLING

STYLIST

A Stylist works together with a photographer, hair stylist, makeup artist, editor, art director, and client to create a look for fashion campaigns (for brands or magazines) fashion shows, lookbooks, and websites (e-commerce stylist), with the goal of making the product as appealing as possible for the final customer. All the looks you see in magazines, lookbooks, advertising campaigns, red carpets, and fashion shows have been studied by the Stylist.

Sometimes fashion editors have a similar role at a fashion magazine, as they are responsible for the look and mood of the shoot, so they choose the photographer, the clothing, the location, and the models.

Celebrity Stylists work with public figures to craft a personal visual aesthetic,
curating their looks for everything from a red carpet event to an everyday coffee run.

ASSISTANT STYLIST

The best way to become a Stylist is to become a Stylist's assistant. The Assistant Stylist supports Stylists in preparing merchandise to be styled and photographed; ensures appropriate products are pulled into the studio and the racks are organized to maximize shooting efficiency; organizes and maintains the workspace and request supplies; receives and sorts any incoming mail for styling division; orders any necessary styling apparel and accessories; tracks and accounts for invoices; manages and organizes styling closets; keeps track of cleaning schedules for product and equipment as well as restocking of styling kits.

TREND FORECASTER

Trend Forecasting is a field that revolves around predicting the future of a market. Trend Forecasters work at magazines, brands, agencies (WGSN one of the most famous).

A Trend Forecaster analyzes data to predict upcoming future trends, colors, styling techniques, fabric textures, and more, that product developers use to create new clothes and accessories for brands.

24

INSIDER TIP:
THE RELATIONSHIPS
BETWEEN FASHION GROUPS

There are thousands of fashion brands out there, but due to their popularity, you can count on your fingers the most popular ones that everyone wants to work for: Gucci, Vogue, Dior, Valentino, and Burberry, are among those.

Getting a job working for these brands is not impossible and with the right strategies you can definitely make it happen, but of course it's more difficult mainly because you have to compete with hundreds and sometimes even thousands of other people. When things get tough it helps to remember this insider tip.

One day when I was still working in the industry, I got an email from the HR department to get access to the Kering portal. I was working on the e-commerce of Alexander McQueen at that time, which is part of that luxury group. In this portal there were job listings from all the brands.

Then one day a colleague of mine moved from one brand to work in another brand within the group, and I immediately thought of the scene from *Confessions of a Shopaholic*, in which the guy at reception tells Rebecca that the job at the fashion magazine was no longer available, but that the financial magazine was hiring. He suggests her to give it a try because both magazines were part of the same group: "Once you're in, you're in," he told her.

And so, a light bulb went on and I realized that that scene in the movie represented the reality of the business.

I also started thinking about other references. Before moving to *Vogue*, Anna Wintour was editor in chief of *House & Garden*, part of the Condè Nast group. It's common that editors move from one magazine to another within the same group.

What I'm trying to say is that considering the relationships between groups is a high-level strategic move.

Vogue could be your ultimate goal, and working at other magazines might be your best bet to get there.

The main groups in fashion are LVMH, Kering, Condè Nast, and Hearst. Some of the brands they include are:

These groups often acquire new brands so I recommend checking their websites for the full and updated list of brands.

LVMH	Kering	Condè Nast	Hearst
Loewe, Louis Vuitton, Dior, Celine, Fendi, Loro Piana, Givenchy, Kenzo, Fenty, Marc Jacobs, Nicholas Kirkwood...	*Gucci, Saint Laurent Balenciaga, Bottega Veneta, Alexander McQueen, Brioni...*	*Architectural Digest Allure, Condé Nast Traveler, Glamour, GQ, House & Garden, La Cucina Italiana, L'uomo, Teen Vogue, The New Yorker, Vanity Fair, Vogue, Vogue Business...*	*Elle, Harper's Bazaar, Marie Claire, Seventeen, Women's Health, O Magazine, Esquire, Town and Country ...*

So if working at *Vogue* is your dream, and you find it difficult to access this publication, why not try working for another publication in the same group?

If you want to work at Gucci, why not consider going to Brioni first and then see if an opportunity opens there?

The LVMH group has different types of brands under its umbrella: from fashion and beauty to wine. You should build experience in a similar brand, so rather than wine just because it's LVMH, consider joining another fashion or jewelry brand depending on what interests you.

This does not mean that the transition will be immediate, you will still have to go through a series of job interviews (even those who change roles or departments in the same company will have to do the interviews again) and an opportunity has to come up, but certainly during the interview you will be considered differently than a stranger and, meanwhile, you are still working for a top brand in the industry, building valuable experience.

25

HOW I TURNED MY INTERNSHIP INTO A PROMOTION

"Ah Giada ... I also wanted to tell you that at the end of these six months there will be no job opportunities. Is it still good for you? "

This was the last question that the HR manager asked me at the end of my interview for my first internship.

With a smile I replied, "Yes, of course!" and inside I thought, "I'll be the best resource and work hard to get a job."

From that moment on, being able to turn that six month internship into something more became a personal challenge.

Six months was enough time and I was confident that something in the company would change during that time; someone not returning from maternity leave, someone else leaving, or simply convincing them that they needed me.

Although obviously I would have preferred to hear that a future career opportunity was awaiting me at the end of the internship or not know anything about my future opportunities, I didn't let that information intimidate or discourage me. In fact, it motivated me.

If you have in your hands an opportunity, or find one that interests you, do not let this kind of situation paralyze you or make you doubt the opportunity. It was my dream job, so even if after six months it was likely going to end, I was going to learn so many things and do what I liked, working for a company I had dreamed about. It would also be a great addition to my CV so I could find something else later.

Being successful in your career doesn't mean getting lucky and avoiding uncomfortable situations or failures. Those who are successful weren't just lucky to have a smooth career path and never encounter difficulties, they simply decided to overcome these challenges.

For five months I worked hard every single day. One month before the internship expired, that same HR Manager and my team manager asked me to meet. They told me they liked me and that they were doing everything they could to find a way for me to stay. Eventually, I stayed there until I left for Glam Observer one year later after I first started.

I want to share with you what I did to turn my internship into a full-time job at the same company where I was initially told there would be no future opportunities. The following tips work, whatever the next step is that you want to achieve, whether it's turning an internship into a full-time job, getting a promotion, taking on more responsibilities, or making a move that will take you to the next level in your career.

Exceed expectations

It doesn't matter if you are still an intern and you are only assigned small tasks. Each assignment or deadline they give you is a new opportunity to show what you can do. Do your best and think about what else you can do, the next step you can take that will make you stand out from all the others. Maybe you can do a task faster than everyone else? Can you add something more? What else can you bring to the table? The better you do anything, the more work they will give you. Do you remember in *The Devil Wears Prada* when Andy not only got copies of the new Harry Potter book, but also bound it, put on the cover, and gave it directly to the girls? Anticipate the needs and next requests of your boss.

Be Proactive

After a month at the company, I understood what my roles and responsibilities were, and I also knew the job of my boss. So every day I organized my schedule and did my job without waiting for my boss to tell me what to do. Every morning I would update her on what I was going to do that day and ask if she had anything else for me or if she wanted me to prioritize something. I am quite a productive person and I get down to work trying to go through all the activities on the list as soon as possible, obviously doing them as best as I can. Generally, every day I was able to finish everything by 6 p.m. My only break was for lunch or to go to the bathroom. One hour before the end of the day I asked my boss if she had anything else for me. I never left work before my boss unless she asked me to. When she had no other jobs for me and I was free, I spent my time studying the tools I was using to manage the e-commerce of the brand to familiarize myself more with the platforms so that I would do my job faster. I was never staring at my hands or checking my phone. When I wasn't studying the tools or creating reports in my free time, I asked other people in the office if they needed help with anything else. Imagine wanting a new job inside your company and the recruiter tells you that unfortunately there are no open positions in your department, but that there is one in a different department and you are qualified because you helped them occasionally and work well with that team! Jackpot! Your chance of turning an internship into a full-time job has doubled or tripled because you're not looking for a full-time job only in your department, but are open to other opportunities elsewhere in that company. And companies certainly prefer to hire those who are already inside and know the company, the products, and the team, rather than hire someone new.

Ask for a promotion

Plan it on time. Don't wait until the last day of your internship to ask about your future.

About a month and a half before your contract expires, talk to your boss and the recruiters. It is super important, from day one, to keep track of everything you do, the goals you have achieved, the projects you have followed, the results you have produced. Get a diary and keep it on your desk in order to write down everything. When weeks and months go by it is difficult to remember what you did, so take notes every day. Prepare a document to show your boss and the recruiter your work over the past weeks and how it has been useful: your article has been viewed x times, social media has grown by x%, remember to your boss how he was excited when you did something extra or reached a goal. I did not do it because they beat me to it, but I would certainly have scheduled a meeting forty-five days before my internship expired if I had not heard from them. I would not have simply said that I would like to stay in the company, but I would have shown them how useful my work was, my contributions, and how well I worked with others.

Be curious and ask questions

Especially when you are at the beginning of your career in fashion, be a learn-it-all, not a know-it-all. Be curious, ask questions, show your interest, absorb as much as possible from everyone. Of course, make sure you ask the questions at the right time, not when your boss is very busy, especially if it's nothing urgent. Consider whether the questions you need answers for are urgent because it's for your job, or if it's something you're curious about and can then discuss during a break.

Be responsible

During my internship, I mainly worked on my laptop all day, so when they asked me to go to the showroom to preview the new collection I was thrilled because I finally could look at clothes and accessories rather than Excel files all day. My boss couldn't go so she asked me to do it and take notes. I was thrilled by the idea of going to the showroom the following day, taking my first taxi alone for a job, and having the responsibility of being the only one there. Unfortunately, that evening my parents called me to tell me that our dog was gone after eleven years. I was devastated and cried all night without falling asleep even for a second. The next morning my eyes were swollen, I felt sad and exhausted, and I was not excited to go to the showroom that morning. Suddenly it didn't seem so fun anymore and all I wanted was to lie in my bed crying for my sweet dog. But my boss was out of town and counting on me; if I didn't go there would be no one from the team there. So I took a shower and got dressed, putting my feelings and priorities aside. With no makeup on I went to the showroom. It was not as fun as I expected but I did it anyway because I felt responsible and I knew it was important for the company.

Being responsible even when you are an intern is essential. Someone told me: "Oh don't worry, you are an intern, take advantage of it!" but I took my job really seriously even if I was just an intern. I was back at work on January 2nd when I could have taken an extra week of vacation, I arrived every day at the office before my boss and always left after they left. I have always considered all my activities, even the simplest ones, as if they were of vital importance for the company.

Make your work essential

The main reason why a company wants you to stay is that your work has become indispensable, so they can't let you go easily because you are a fundamental part of the team. Think about it in advance and not just in the last two days before your contract or internship expires. From the day you walk into the office to the moment you become familiar with your activities, do them as best as you can and, over time, ask for more tasks so that you gain more responsibility. It doesn't matter if you are a trainee, practical tasks are important and can become indispensable. Getting out of your comfort zone and asking for more work helps you to build experience and increases your value within the company. After the first weeks of my internship, when I understood my job, I tried to become independent. I searched for many Excel formulas on Google or tried to figure out a solution by myself and asked for help only when I couldn't find anything.

Never say that something is not your responsibility or that you are unable to do it. There is always a solution to everything, and you are the person who will manage to figure it out.

Work Hard

Obviously, the #1 rule to get noticed in a fashion office is to work hard. Be a hard worker, give 101% in every assignment, and never be the person who has nothing to do. When you are done, ask for more work, and ask people from other departments if necessary. Make sure you are always busy and if no one has work for you to do, as I suggested before, work on something yourself: analyze the competitors, see if you can propose a new project for the company or a process that can be automated or improved, arrange the spaces, organize the wardrobe ... Don't procrastinate and always bring the best results as quickly as possible!

Think like a boss

I think that one of the factors that contributed the most to the success of my internship was the fact that I already had an entrepreneurial mindset, even when I was not working for my company yet. I cared about the company as if it were mine, therefore having a totally different vision and attitude. If I had to stay late to finish, I stayed. I thought about how to improve processes and did whatever it took to make the team and the brand successful. I brought the work laptop with me over the summer despite the fact that I was just an intern and it wasn't requested, and one day my boss couldn't do something, so I offered to do it. It was a day in August during vacation that I launched the sales for the online store. Many might have thought that just because it wasn't my responsibility, I shouldn't care and leave my boss to find a solution. But this mentality has never taken anyone far. I offered to do it without anyone asking me. Consider the company where you work as if it were your own. Don't just do the bare necessities, don't be passive, and don't go to the office like you're just going to spend those eight hours mindlessly. If you consider the company as if it were your own and work hard, putting passion and commitment into it and being proactive will come to you spontaneously. Each milestone of the company will also be yours and you will feel like you're part of its success.

Learn, grow, and ask for more

Having more skills is essential if you want to grow. If there is anything this pandemic has taught us it is that things can change very quickly and the people who have been able to survive are those who are able to adapt and be flexible. If you want to grow and be flexible, never stop learning something new. If you want to take on more responsibility, you need to learn more skills, and you can acquire these skills by learning something new every day on your own. Learning new things immediately gives us more confidence to ask for more at work. Don't wait for your boss to ask you to take on additional responsibilities. Did you take a User Experience course? Ask your boss if you can help out with the UX design for the company. Have you taken a course and learned something new that the company is not already doing? Don't be afraid to propose it to your boss.

Set a goal to take a new online course every month to keep learning, stay inspired, and grow your skills! Even if you think it's something you don't necessarily need now, everything you learn contributes to your persona and sooner or later you will apply everything you learn.

Earn their trust

It's super important to be fair and honest. Earning the trust of your boss and your team is greatly satisfying. If you want a promotion, more responsibility, or a change of role, you must first earn their trust. They must be sure that every job you take on, you will do in the best possible way, and with honesty; not only towards the company but also towards the external people with whom you will have to deal with. As an employer, you represent the brand everywhere you go and with anyone you talk to outside of your company.

CONCLUSION

YOU ARE THE FUTURE OF THE FASHION INDUSTRY

D<small>ear reader,</small>

You are the future of the fashion industry.

We have the responsibility to make one of the best industries in the world, even better.

A place where everyone feels appreciated, a place where everyone feels represented, a place that respects everyone's working conditions: from those who collect cotton in the fields, to those who work in factories, stores, agencies, and offices. An industry that not only respects people, but also our beautiful world because without it we are nothing. A place full of as many beautiful dresses as beautiful people. An industry that unites, an industry full of creativity and talent. An industry that excites and makes you dream: the happy sigh before entering the office for the first time, the beating of a heart before an interview, the silence before a fashion show, the lights that start a catwalk, the sound of applause at the end, the window shopping, the admiration for those who made history, and the enthusiasm for the talents of today and tomorrow. An industry that, although increasingly digital, is still humanly connected. A fast industry that always looks forward but at the same time has reverence for its past. A sector that renews and does not waste.

Fashion is up to you. And as I have faith in the future of fashion, I have faith in you. I trust that from now on, you will believe in yourself. You promised me, remember?

I believe you are aware that there will be challenges, but that you'll choose to be strong and won't give up. You are special, and the fashion industry and the world needs a valuable asset like you. I'm confident that every day you will do something that will take you where you want to go and that you will live your life to the fullest, without excuses, without prejudices. Remember to have fun in the process; from your first internship, to your job search, to your promotion. Celebrate your achievements but don't condemn failures.

Keep dreaming and making plans!

We have reached the end of this journey together. I'm almost crying. I used to write every day for so long thinking of you. But we can continue this journey together if you want to. You will find my articles on glamobserver.com, you can listen to The Glam Observer Podcast, take one or all of the courses, and hug us at an event or virtually in a webinar or event on Zoom.

See you soon,

Giada

ABOUT THE AUTHOR

Giada Graziano is a fashion career expert, online educator, speaker, podcaster, entrepreneur and now author of her first book
Your Fashion [Dream] Plan.
She is the Founder and CEO of Glam Observer
the top-rated fashion career advice platform that through articles, podcasts, events, and courses supports and inspires those who want to start a career in fashion.

In 2020 Giada entered the Forbes Under 30 list in the Education category for empowering the future of the fashion industry through her platform, career advice and courses.
Over the past six years Giada has mentored and helped thousands of fashion enthusiasts from all over the world getting a job in fashion.
Her work has been featured on Forbes, Marie Claire, Elle...
To find more about all the things head over to glamobserver.com